Mountain Friends

Joe Mitchell

ISBN-13: 9781537687643

DEDICATION AND ACKNOWLEDGEMENTS

This book is dedicated to anyone who has ever been on a church missions committee and prayed for someone on the other side of the globe.

Thanks to my friends at the annual BivWhack for giving me the encouragement to start this project, and to my friends at Walsh Engineering for giving me the time off work to complete it. It was more difficult and more fun than I anticipated.

Thanks to Kim, Anna, Niels, Evan, Michaila, Joel, Michelle, Lori, Brandy, Ruth, Leanna, Dave, Stephanie, Nancy, and Dave for reading the full text and providing valuable feedback. I take full responsibility for the remaining errors and questionable taste.

Finally, thanks to my wife Kim; she taught me about semicolons and forgiveness.

CONTENTS

VISUAL PROLOGUE

These photos are included to provide a visual context for the stories that follow. But feel free to visualize in full color.

A Tibetan grandmother.

A young Nosu man.

Nosu girls.

Inside a village school.

Tibetan schoolboys.

High school students at mandatory morning exercises.

Tibetan monks at a ghost dance.

A fisherman on Lugu Lake.

Tibetan high school students performing a traditional dance.

A village pig meets his destiny.

Joe Mitchell

Students performing on Parent's Day.

A Tibetan mastiff with his owner.

Yak hybrids used as a team to skid beams.

Using a crosscut saw to shape beams for stone post-and-beam house construction.

A typical Tibetan village home, with rammed earth, post-and-beam construction. The ground floor is used for livestock, the second floor for the family, and the third floor for drying produce.

Typical Nosu style log cabin construction.

Joe Mitchell

A temporary cabin used during summer pasture season.

A yak near Tiger Leaping Gorge.

Joe Mitchell

Tibetan stupas and prayer flags near Kawagebo.

Tibetan Buddhist artwork in a monastery.

Stone, wood, and clay tile construction.

AUTHOR'S NOTE AND INTRODUCTION

My wife Kim and I have lived in China off and on for a total of seven years beginning in 1993. During three of those years we lived on a one-acre property with a minority Nosu family. The occupants of the property included our family of four, their family of five, up to 20 pigs, six dogs, many visitors, and a chaotic stream of their extended family. Our two kids, Anna and Niels, spent time with their kids every day, and we shared life together.

Everything in this book actually happened. I have used nicknames for people and omitted some place names so that nothing I have written could cause problems for anyone I have mentioned. All of the photos are from the actual events described. All of the conversations with people in China were in Chinese, so the quotations are my translations. My Chinese isn't perfect so I'm sure the quotations aren't either. But I did write down most of the stories soon after they happened, so they are not also casualties of memory reconstruction. There are some composite conversations, but no composite characters.

I wrote the book to tell our stories. If it also happens to make money, half of the profits I receive will go toward medical care and education for Nosu children. The other half will probably go toward medical care for Kim and me; we're not getting any younger.

Joe Mitchell—Plummer, Idaho, 2017.

Joe Mitchell

1 LITTLE BIRD

"Do you not know that I am a woman? When I think, I must speak!" Rosalind, in Shakespeare's As You Like It.

When Kim and I met Little Bird and her mother, Ahma, in 2004, they were living in a tiny shack, trying to make ends meet by recycling bottles and selling pitchwood. We very much wanted to get connected with some Nosu people so we offered Little Bird a job as our everyday cook and language tutor. When we told them the going rate for that job—$10 per month—their eyes widened and filled with tears. "No, it's too much!"

Little Bird was 19. She was beautiful in an athletic way, slim with wide shoulders and big hands. If you had met her in the US you could imagine she was a foreign college student with a scholarship in a niche sport, like doubles crew.

Ahma was in her late 40s, an illiterate village grandmother[1] who was intelligent and mischievous. She always wore her traditional ethnic clothes, including a square black hat, huge, like a graduation cap on steroids. She was strong and capable. Once I watched a skinny Singaporean man and a soft Indian man work together to carry a full 50-liter water barrel a few yards,

---

[1] Ahma is the Nosu word for grandmother. It was one of the few Nosu words I could pronounce perfectly. The word for grandfather is Ahpu, and my Nosu friends said I also pronounced it correctly, but only when I sneezed.

sweating and grunting. Ahma picked it up by herself and carried it back, throwing her head back in laughter.

Little Bird and Ahma each misled us about their marital status, like the woman at the well in the Bible. Ahma said she was widowed, when in fact she had an ex-husband who lived in town with his mistress.

Little Bird said she was unmarried, but actually she had just completed a village ceremony with a 14-year-old.

If you met her husband in the US, you might think he was a spoiled 8th grader who ate too many cupcakes and played too many video games. He was actually the golden boy in his village, the #1 student in his school, and the hope of his clan.

Ahma's clan had just settled a long standing financial debt to his clan by giving Little Bird to him as a wife. Little Bird hated the idea, protested, tried to run away; but by clannish coercion, cajoling and threats, she finally went through with the ceremonial wedding. We were told they wouldn't sleep together until he turned 17, and they would probably never get a Chinese marriage license.

If you imagine a chubby 8th grader you know, just married to an attractive college girl you know, you can imagine the expression on this boy's face. The young husband had a stupid, complacent smile that didn't leave for months. Little Bird derisively called him Little Brother, made fun of him, but did admit he was good at math.

Little Bird had a 6th grade education, but was a PhD at understanding bad Chinese. We talked with her for hours the first few months we were learning, and she at least pretended to understand everything we said. She never laughed at us, never used baby talk, and would paraphrase her own stories with vocabulary we could understand.

Just after we met her, when we knew almost no Chinese at all, we went for a walk. I had my vocabulary notebook at the ready. We saw a colorful bird, possibly a red-billed blue magpie. I asked her what it was called and carefully wrote down her reply "*xiao niao*". Later we saw a finch and I asked her what it was called. Oddly, she gave the same reply. How could she mix up a magpie and a finch? Later, I used my dictionary to identify my vocabulary notebook entries. Knowing my limited grasp of the language, she had called each one "a little bird." We laughed, and her nickname stuck.

She cooked for us for three years, before our roles changed and she became our landlord. She spent her own money to buy a cookbook and became fast and competent. Nosu people traditionally spend most waking hours working outdoors in the high altitude sun and need to consume copious amounts of salt. She would pour salt out of a bag into her hand and throw it in the potatoes, meat, vegetables, and soup. We bought her a shaker for tighter salt control, but she would still take the lid off, pour out a handful, and dump it in.

She was the best liar I have ever met. When we traveled together she got us past checkpoints and got deep discounts on everything we needed with a bewildering blast of improvised stories. When she worked for us and asked for time off, sometimes I would ask her, "Why *do* you want time off tomorrow?" not because I thought I might say no, but just to hear the extravagant creativity of her excuse.

Her job with us only required 2-3 hours per day, and she was a hyperactive entrepreneur. She ran a food cart, a firewood business ("it's totally legal, but we take the truck through the checkpoint at 3 AM and bring snacks for the guards, just as a precaution"), a beauty salon, a real estate business, an ad-hoc travel agency, and a guesthouse. Plus she repaired cars, raised pigs, grew maca, and flipped any commodity she could find. Once I returned home to find my outdoor basketball court filled with 30 mattresses from a hotel, another time with two tons of charcoal in pig food bags.

One night she called my cell. "Mr. Mitchell, do you know how to drive?"

"Of course. Pretty much every American adult knows how."

"That's great, because I just bought a car, and I don't. Could you ride your bicycle out and drive it home for me?"

It was a beat up Isuzu pickup, 4-cylinder, 5-speed manual transmission, no power steering. The next day I took her out to a deserted part of the grassland to learn to drive. She popped the clutch and spun out in the dirt. She bounced off the trail into the ditch. I had never driven a car in China and didn't know the names of the accelerator, brake, clutch, or steering wheel. I gave her directions like Vizzini captaining his sailing ship in the movie *Princess Bride*. "Now step on that thing! Quick, the other thing!"

When we finished, she drove like a person who just had their first driving lesson—which is to say, she was a significant hazard to herself and anything within 50 meters of the road. I said, "That was great for a first lesson. Let's go back tomorrow and you can work on letting out that one thing more smoothly, and stepping on that other thing not quite so fast. And today you only got to 1, 2, and 3. Tomorrow we'll use 4, 5, and R."

She laughed. "No time for more lessons. I've got stuff to pick up in Kunming tomorrow." Kunming was 12 hours of steep descents and hairpin curves away.

Always the practical engineer, I raised some objections. "But you don't have a driver's license, and your Isuzu doesn't have plates yet. Also, remember, you don't know how to drive."

"No worries. You taught me enough. And my brother said that if you find a big truck to follow you can tuck in behind it so close the police won't even notice you."

She arrived home four days later, pickup bed filled with merchandise to sell, an expert driver.

Little Bird.

2 REZ BALL

"And I realized that, sure, Indians were drunk and sad and displaced and crazy and mean, but dang, we knew how to laugh." Sherman Alexie, The Absolutely True Diary of a Part-time Indian

I grew up on the Coeur d' Alene Indian Reservation in Northern Idaho. Plummer High School had some of the worst standardized test scores in the state, but we were good at basketball. My senior year I was a finalist for North Idaho Athlete of the Year.[2] I liked growing up on the rez.

The minority areas in China resemble Indian reservations in the states. People aren't obsessed with productivity or taking their kid to three kinds of lessons every day, so there is ample time for boredom and friendships to develop. People are poor, and they place a high value on humor. Of course humor is a coping mechanism for poverty and alcoholism and unemployment and divorce. But to some degree it works.

Basketball rivals soccer as the sports obsession of poor minority people everywhere, from Tibet to Lagos to Oaxaca. It is cheap to play, and it values physical courage and the willingness to get knocked down. I think the aggressive

---

[2] I'm not only bragging like Uncle Rico in the movie *Napoleon Dynamite*; this is also necessary background for the chapter.

showmanship and physical valor in basketball replaces the roles that males used to have in traditional cultures, like hunting and stealing and fighting.

One school in China where Kim and I taught English had a team of mostly Han Chinese teachers that had played together for years. They played teams of teachers from other local schools. They heard I could ball and asked me to join. I was better than they were and they didn't like me to steal their show, so after a couple of games they stopped inviting me. But if they were playing a good team and got behind, they would call me. "Can you come right now? The Benzilan Tibetan Middle School teachers are killing us!"

So I played the second half of the games, if my team got behind. When we played the Benzilan Tibetans, I scored the first few possessions after halftime, and they started to just tackle and hold me in the backcourt. One guy grabbed me, and when I spun away from him, I accidentally nailed a different Tibetan in the nose with my elbow. I felt the bones and cartilage give way, and blood poured.

If this had happened in a city-league game in Idaho Falls, Idaho, an ambulance would have been called, a cousin of the injured guy would have threatened to take out my knees, and I would have also been threatened with a lawsuit.

But the Tibetans thought it was hilarious! Including the one with the broken nose. The referees stopped play so they could laugh. It was an outdoor court and the injured guy went to the sideline, stuffed wads of grass up both sides of his nose and kept playing, red blood dripping off the ends of the green grass.

After the game the Tibetans gathered around me so that we could all laugh some more. "That was so funny when your long arm swung around and broke his nose!" and, "We have a saying that if you have long arms, your other body parts are also long. Is that true for Americans?" (Embarrassed silence from me—I didn't even know all the vocabulary words in Chinese—and more laughter from them.) The injured guy asked me where we lived, and after that sometimes when he came through town he would stop to visit, and we became friends.

I can't remember who won that game. I can remember the

thin air at 10,500 feet, and the thin blue sky, and the white clouds, and the white mountains, and the brown Tibetan men, and basketball, and laughter.

3 SITTING ON THE BRIDE

"By all means marry. If you get a good wife, you'll become happy; if you get a bad one, you'll become a philosopher."
Socrates

The 17-year-old Nosu girl was brought to the groom's mountainous village by some of her male relatives; no female friends or relatives were allowed to attend. She wore traditional bridal clothes including heavy silver jewelry. She was carsick and appeared to be in a state of shock. She was crying with a blanket over her face, not speaking to anyone.

Family and friends, all Nosu except for my family, began arriving and animals were being butchered for the first meal. Guests paid their respects to the oldest member of the groom's family with gifts of meat, liquor, and cigarettes. Most of the women wore traditional colored skirts and big black hats. Like any other large village gathering, there was a system where each guest gave some money to the hosts to help with the expenses.

Later, we sat outdoors on a grassy hillside, in a circle around a fire-pit with some other guests, talking. The air and the ground were cold at 10,000 feet so I sat on a pile of wool blankets. I was wondering when we would be introduced to the bride and then something moved under me and I realized, "Oh no, I'm sitting on her!" She was lying silently under that pile of blankets, and I thought she was a couch.[3]

Later that evening when the first star came out, a temporary shelter was built of poles and bamboo mats. The bride's family carried her into the shelter and ate a ceremonial meal with the groom's family. The meal included turnips, liquor, and pig feet. In a separate ceremony, the groom's family fed him a special meal in which the most important element was a sheep's tongue.

When the ceremony ended, the temporary shelter was promptly torn down, and all of the guests went back to the host's house. There were fires flaring in indoor and outdoor fire-pits. Each group of guests was given large chunks of pork and buckwheat bread dough. We were told to find a fire and put the food directly in the coals to cook it—no pots or pans were allowed for this meal.

Later, everyone crowded into the largest available room. The guests were offered liquor, beer, candy, sunflower seeds, and cigarettes. The men were sitting on one side of the room, the women on the other, haphazardly. The oldest or most important male members of the bride's and groom's families had the seats of honor, behind the fire.

Two men from the groom's family started a kind of memorized dialogue. They sounded like rappers. One of them was holding a tray with two bowls of liquor and some money. They said, 'Where is the bride's uncle?' 'I think he's over there.' 'Is that the bride's uncle?' 'I think he's over here.' Every time one of the men said, 'I think he's over there,' the man with the tray handed it to one of the guests who said, 'No, I'm not the uncle,' until he finally handed it to the correct person. The uncle poured the liquor from one bowl to the other—symbolizing the unity of the two families—drank it, and took the money from the tray. Then the "rapper" carried the tray back to refill it. As he did so he imitated an animal, symbolizing one of the animals that can be slaughtered at a wedding ceremony. One time he bleated like a lamb, another he bellowed like a bull. He was gifted at animal imitations and he had the whole room in fits of

---

[3] Later, when our local friends were telling stories, someone would always say, "Hey, have you guys heard the one about the foreigner sitting on the bride?"

laughter.

Each of the adult male guests was given a cigarette to smoke together, also showing unity. I was sitting by the groom's father. He had been translating the Nosu language to Chinese for me during the ceremonies. He said, "I know you don't normally smoke, but you should this time, it is part of the ceremony." So at age 40, in a room filled with wood smoke from an open fire, surrounded by people who already smelled like various kinds of smoke, I had my first cigarette.

We were told that at most weddings there is a lively singing contest between the bride's and groom's families. At this one there was a desultory attempt to get it started, but it never really got going. Like most other Nosu gatherings, the young people got out a boombox and did some line dancing. Then everyone went to bed.

The next day another pig was killed and all of the guests ate together again. I had noticed that the groom did not attend any part of the ceremony where the bride was present. I asked as delicately as I could about when the bride and groom would start to share a room. Everyone laughed and one lady said, "They still haven't met! If they are both really shy they may not even speak to each other for a long time. It may be months before they share a room!"

Many new brides try to escape after the guests leave, depending on their first impression of their new husband. They usually try to find their way back to their home village, or try to lose themselves in a big city like Kunming. In this wedding, the groom had a physical disability (a hunchback, that we were told had been caused by tuberculosis, which was common in that area) that the bride was unaware of, and it was widely expected that she would try to run off after she found out. Then it would be the responsibility of the groom's family to find her and bring her back, if necessary by force. Many new brides are beaten or locked up after an attempt to run off. Suicides are not uncommon. Occasionally her own family will take her back and pay reparation, or defy the groom's family and start a feud. Sometimes the couple reaches an uneasy long-term truce, and sometimes they learn to love and appreciate each other.

Three days after the wedding, when the bride and groom finally mustered the courage to meet, they liked each other. Really well! It wasn't months before they started sharing a room.

Sheep says, "baaaaaa!"

4 BACKSTORY

"All happy families are alike, each unhappy family is unhappy in its own way." Leo Tolstoy, Anna Karenina

Kim and I weren't always bumbling through China, breaking the noses of unwary Tibetans and sitting on unhappy brides. In 1986 we were attending the University of Idaho, busily falling in love.

Our first conversation was outdoors, and we talked about growing up poor, not really caring about money or the American Dream, and wanting to live overseas, maybe in China. Kim was idealistic and looked great in faded jeans and a flannel shirt. I told a friend that she combined the best qualities of Ellie May Clampett and Mother Theresa.

A photograph from that fall shows us on our first date, deer hunting. We were bareheaded and each grabbing our rifles with one hand, laughing, full of *joie de vivre*. We had a June wedding.

While working out a just-married-budget, I suggested to Kim that my $4,000 in student loans were low-interest and we just pay the minimum. She had worked her way through college debt-free, and suggested we pay them off as fast as possible and be financially free. Three months later we were free indeed.

The next five years I worked as an electrical engineer at the Idaho National Laboratory in Southeast Idaho. Kim taught English and Spanish at Sand Creek Middle School. We spent two evenings a week helping lead a church youth group that sometimes swelled to 100 teenagers. We bought an International Scout for $1,600 and a small old farmhouse for $16,000.

We backpacked, skied, hunted, and fished most weekends. We didn't have a mortgage, a car payment, a kid, or a care. One weekend we were waiting out a rainstorm in our backpack tent in the Sawtooth wilderness. One of us said, "We are in our late twenties, should we start thinking about having kids?"

We looked at each other, laughed, and said, "Nah, let's go to China instead."

In 1993 the internet was used for military email, FTP downloads, and probably Trekkie newsgroups. Finding a distant job was a crude and painful process involving telephones and large manila envelopes. But we set out to find work overseas.

Kim and I are unredeemed goal setters and list makers. We have written out 5 year goals every 3 years we have been married, with 12 categories like Physical, Financial, Educational, etc. Our written goals at that time for working overseas were:

• Live in a non-Western culture.

• Spend most of our time with local people. So teaching at an international school, with the entitled children of diplomats, and quirky children of missionaries, was out.

• Have the opportunity to explain who Jesus is to people who had never heard of Him[4].

We joined up with Educational Services International, who matched American college graduates with teaching positions in China. At the end of 6 six weeks of English as a Second Language (ESL) training in Pasadena, 70 of us flew to Asia. Our teaching assignment was in Chongqing, in the Sichuan basin. I overlaid a map of the Sichuan basin on a map of Idaho, and although there were 100 times more people, the map didn't even cover above McCall. We were leaving one of the emptiest parts of the planet for one of the fullest.

When you de-plane, the first thing you notice about China is the smell. It is charcoal smoke, diesel exhaust, burnt red

---

[4] Kim and I are evangelical Christians. If that is a problem, better stop reading here, it gets worse. You could still give the book 5 stars on Amazon to show you are open-minded.

peppers, and old urine. Eventually you can recognize regional variations: Beijing has more smoke, Shanghai more exhaust, Guangzhou more urine.

All the teachers went to Beijing together, ate roast duck, watched contortionist acrobats, went to the Great Wall, and had a meeting with a Communist official. She welcomed us warmly and warned us not to talk about religion or politics in our classrooms.

About 50 times more Americans visit China each year now than 25 years ago, and we all thought we were privileged to be part of something special and exotic.

Chongqing was exotic, in a Sichuan basin backwater kind of way. It had not yet become a national municipality and gateway to western China. The Three Gorges Dam project had not started construction yet. It was in the heart of old-school Chinese China, like an illustration from *Ping the Duck*. There were short day-laborers with rolled up dirty blue pants carrying their ban-ban poles. Old women whose feet had been bound as girls argued about the price of vegetables.[5] Memories of the Cultural Revolution were recent and conversations were usually guarded.

We taught English at the Chongqing Civil Engineering Institute. It was at the 7 km mark on the road out of town to the east. A 15-minute walk around rice paddies, carp ponds, and vegetable gardens took us to the Yangtze River.

We were a novelty in our part of town and crowds would gather, staring, whenever we stopped. Once Kim went into a dress-maker's shop to buy a *qipao*, a traditional long gown, and I waited outside. A fascinated group of about 40 people stood outside the shop. The lady tailor took Kim's measurements. She called out, "90, 65, 90[6]!" and there were gasps of appreciation and wonder.

Sometimes, on a bad day, we tired of attention from the crowds, but we loved our students. Most of them were young engineering professors who had been released from teaching

---

[5] Old Sichuan women arguing about the price of vegetables sounds like road construction.

[6] Keep in mind, China uses the metric system.

their classes for a semester to study English with us. We had four hours each day in the classroom. Outside of class we ate meals in the students' apartments, played basketball and ping-pong, and began to talk freely, even about politics and religion. (At that time Kim and I only knew travel Chinese so these conversations were all in English.) Once we checked our calendar and observed we had just completed 42 consecutive days with a dinner invitation or other social outing. We had no expat friends, so we spent the year immersed in Chinese culture. Here are some of the things we learned:

• The American lifestyle is not the only one that works. We had thought that we were counter-cultural because we were out of debt and not in love with what we owned. But we had still bought into the hyper-individuality of American life.

• Friendships were more important than we had realized. Our Chongqing friends loaned each other money, helped discipline each other's kids, saw each other almost every day, but were open enough to include us in their friendship group.

• Good food is worth the effort. Chongqing is in the heart of the traditional Sichuan food culture and we loved it. Once I told our friends, "I can't speak much Chinese. I have never been able to keep the dynasties straight. Chinese books and movies are inscrutable. But I love Chinese food, and I can eat more of it than any of you!"

They laughed and said, "You have learned the most important part of our culture."

• Comparing my attitudes in Idaho and China showed my hypocrisy. I showed tremendous grace to Chinese people and culture, was grateful for the opportunity to be there, and never spoke an unkind word. The previous five years in Idaho Falls, in the predominantly Mormon culture, I had shown no grace, complained about living there, and made unfunny Mormon jokes behind their backs. The contrast was convicting, I changed, and life in Idaho improved dramatically.

Living in China for that year had a profound and positive impact on our lives. One of the impacts was to light a slow burning fuse that would eventually result in our connection with the Nosu people. Like our first decision to go to China, our connection with the Nosu began with a camping trip.

The university where we taught took a two-month winter break for Chinese New Year. We used the time to camp and hike in Yunnan province. Tiger Leaping Gorge has class VI whitewater, unclimbed peaks, and some of the world's most spectacular scenery. While camping near there, a grandmother in an enormous black hat invited us to stay with her family. They didn't speak any English or Chinese so we smiled and gestured and played with the kids for a couple of days. A pretty teenage mother had images of coins (money to spend in the after-life) tattooed on her arm. The young father coughed incessantly. They had a fire in the middle of their log cabin, without a stove or chimney. We ate potatoes baked in the ashes and shared our chocolate. They were really poor; we didn't eat anything *except* potatoes. I told Kim, "This was a great cultural exchange. We gave them tooth decay from the chocolate, they gave us TB." Despite my sarcasm we felt an immediate connection with that gritty family.

A life altering dinner invitation.

After returning to Idaho, Kim and I had great memories, but no plans to ever return to China, except for short visits to see our Chongqing friends. We were also uncertain about ever having kids. We liked our life together, liked to travel, and didn't see the need. We asked our pastor, Dave Gibson, for his advice.

He said, "I can't give you a verse from the Bible that commands it now that the earth is full. I can't give you a logical argument that will convince you. But trust me, you should have kids." We did trust him, and about 4 hours and 9 months later Anna was born.

Another couple of years later we had another fast drive to the hospital, and as a baby's head emerged, the doctor asked me, "Do these look like girl's ears or boy's ears?"

I said, "I can't tell from the ears." A few seconds later we could tell, as our son Niels was born.

We were one of Tolstoy's happy families, doing the things that other happy families do: lots of couch time with good children's books, outdoor play dates with friends and sticks and water, wrestling on the carpet, date nights with Kim. We made chocolate banana pancakes every Saturday morning, and had popcorn with our read-alouds almost every evening. I worked a three day week as an engineer, and we had adequate money for the four day weekends. Kim became a legendary home school mom. We were active at church and had more great friends than we deserved. People said we had life wired. We didn't disagree.

One of my roles at church was leader of the missions team. In the mid 90's there was a movement for churches to "adopt an unreached people group." In Christian missions, "unreached" means that there are less than 2% believers, and no natural means of coming to faith without intentional effort by missions organizations. Adopt meant to have a long term commitment. (I always thought "adopting" a people group sounded patronizing, and I don't think that phrase is used much now.) Our elder board put out a Request For Proposal to the missions team. "Give us four people group adoption proposals, and we'll choose." Kim, recalling a memory of that dinner from years ago, suggested we should submit the Chinese minority that had hosted us. We did some research and learned they were Nosu, a subset of the Yi, one of the 55 registered Chinese minorities. I wrote the proposal.

The four proposals that were submitted to the elders were:
- The Nosu of China

- The Bengali Muslims
- The Dominicans
- The Mormons[7]

The elder board chose the Nosu of China. As missions team leader I began to make contacts. After months of emails, calls, and conferences, I had found opportunities to go to more conferences and network, but none to do what we really wanted to do, which was to connect with Nosu people, like we had years before in the Yunnan mountains.

Kim and I began to get frustrated with the missionaries in the cities and their supervisors in the US. "What's wrong with these people? Everyone just wants to network and coordinate strategy and go to conferences in Thailand[8]. Nobody is *willing* to go live in the Mountains and make Friends."

God made an unexpected entry into our story and said, "Are *you* willing?"

---

[7] I suspect the Mormons reading this are saying, "The 600 people in your evangelical community church were seriously going to *adopt* 11 million Mormons? You cocky bastards!" Except that Mormons don't swear.

[8] Conferences in Thailand are a blast.

5 BAYES AND THE TOMB

"Bayes theorem is concerned with conditional probability. That is, it tells us the probability that a theory or hypothesis is true if some event has happened." Nate Silver, The Signal and the Noise.

This book is filed as non-fiction, and to have God suddenly enter the story requires some explanation. If you are already a believer, you could skip this chapter; but I know you won't, because you'll want to do fact-checking.

My favorite phrase when my kids asked me a question was "What's the evidence?" I believe the evidence for it being possible for God to enter my story is:

1. People are a bewildering combination of awesomeness, beauty, stupidity, reverence, lust, altruism, and evil. The best explanation I have heard for this is the Christian doctrine of people being created in God's image, then rebelling against God by falling into sin.

2. Almost all people, in all cultures, in all of history, have a numinous awe of the supernatural—unless they have it sucked out of them, like by daily instruction in Communist public schools, or by watching too many just-believe-in-*yourself* Hollywood movies.

3. Most of us long to be forgiven of our badness, even as we protest our innocence, like the prisoners do in the movie *The*

Shawshank Redemption.

4. Jesus was a historical person who claimed to be able to forgive sin, like ours.

5. Jesus came back from the dead, according to the Old Testament scriptures, as he predicted. The historical resurrection is the ultimate Evidence.

6. When people give up on trusting in themselves and begin to trust in Jesus, good things happen—like peace, joy, contentment, repaired relationships, a sigh of relief that their sins have been forgiven, better treatment of women and children, a better work ethic, hospitals, schools, and happy families. None of these things is unique to Christianity, and none will be perfect, but there will be measureable and substantial change.

7. I had a personal sense of my own badness and a need for forgiveness. Believing that Jesus' death on the cross had paid the penalty for my badness gave me a sense of peace. I don't believe the sense of peace was self-help auto-suggestion vaporware; I believe there had been an actual forgiveness of my sins that changed my life.

8. Independently from me, Kim had essentially the same experience[9].

Using Bayesian inference (which I attempt to explain at the end of this chapter) if your starting point is 100% certainty, you will never change your mind, regardless of any new evidence. This applies to certainty that God does not exist and could not have given direction to Kim and me, as much as to certainty that he does and could. I am a natural skeptic and have never had 100% certainty of anything, instead letting new evidence continually adjust my beliefs. And the evidence I have seen is that God is there and He is not silent.

Of course Christianity is not primarily a logic problem to solve. It is primarily a response to history's most compelling individual, Jesus Christ. Even as a baby he was a polarizing figure, with wise men bowing down to him and a king trying to murder him. He divides people into two camps, and neither will

---

[9] In general, Kim is a more reliable person than I am.

fully understand the other.

The Spirit blows wherever it wants to and there is a mystery to faith and revelation. It is mysterious but real, and non-fiction.

For engineers and scientists, one method of continually updating your confidence in a hypothesis, after accounting for new evidence, is called Bayesian inference. It provides a mathematical basis for the updates. Following is some optional background on Bayesian inference. I believe that it helps illustrate the response all of us have to new evidence, including the evidence for Christian faith, but it is not central to the story, so if you want to, you can skip ahead to the next chapter with a clear conscience.

Thomas Bayes was a Presbyterian minister and mathematician who lived in England in the 18th century. He is best known for developing Bayes Theorem, which was published after his death. When Bayes theorem is applied to probabilities, it is called Bayesian inference.

We all intuitively use Bayesian inference, as we decide things like how likely it is a girl will say "yes" when we ask her out (that smile yesterday was definitely new evidence!) or when we decide whether to pack a raincoat. Mathematically, here is how it works:

U is the updated probability of the hypothesis, after seeing the new evidence.

X is the initial probability of the hypothesis, called the "prior".

Y is the probability the hypothesis is shown to be true, given the new evidence.

Z is the probability the hypothesis is shown to be false, given the new evidence.

$$U = X * \frac{Y}{X * Y + Z(1 - X)}$$

Example 1 – Flyfishing.

My hypothesis is that Wooly Buggers will out-fish Dave's Hoppers on the South Fork of the Snake. I'm 60% certain that this is true. The new evidence is that at the end of the day, my friend had caught 12 trout on hoppers, and I had caught only one on a bugger.

Maybe my friend had better presentation, or a smaller tippet, or maybe I was rowing during the best water, so I allow some room for uncertainty, giving an 80% chance that the day's results refute my hypothesis, and a 20% chance that it doesn't. So Z is 0.8, Y is 0.2, and X (my prior) is 0.6. Solving,

$$U = .6 * \frac{.2}{.6 * .2 + .8(1 - .6)} = .27$$

Considering the new evidence, I am now only 27% certain that my fly is the best choice, but I don't change flies, and we have the same results again. Now,

$$U = .27 * \frac{.2}{.27 * .2 + .8(1 - .27)} = 0.08$$

After two days fishing, I think there is only an 8% chance that my favorite fly will work better than his tomorrow, so I pull out my vise and deer hair, and start tying some hoppers.

Example 2 – Evolution.

Archie believes that animals cannot evolve across family lines–a cat cannot change into a dog. He is 100% certain that this hypothesis is true. The new evidence is that scientists at Beijing University have developed methods to mutate and breed salamanders, and within 20 generations, they are able to reliably change salamanders into any kind of animal in the Beijing zoo, including adorable giant pandas.

Let's say there is a 99% chance this new evidence refutes Archie's hypothesis, so Z=.99, Y=.01, and X =1.

Archie now believes the probability there is no way for cats to evolve into dogs is:

$$U = 1 * \frac{.99}{1 * .99 + .99(1 - 1)} = 1$$

The new evidence did not weaken his belief at all! Since he was 100% convinced of his initial hypothesis, no amount of new evidence will ever change his certainty that his beliefs are true.

In one of Jesus' parables he said, "If they won't listen to Moses and the prophets, they won't listen even if someone rises from the dead!" If he had been talking only to a group of engineers and scientists (brows furrowed, dutifully taking notes) he might have said, 'If they didn't leave some room in their priors for new evidence to adjust their estimate of the certainty of their hypotheses, no new evidence, no matter how compelling, will ever get them to change their minds!'

It may seem counter-intuitive that a Christian, like me, would advocate leaving some room for doubt. But I believe Christianity can endure evaluation of all available evidence, so set your priors greater than 0, less than 100, and go for it!

We now return to the story…

6 MOUNTAIN FRIENDS

"For whoever would save their life will lose it, but whoever loses their life for me will save it." Jesus

The idea that God wanted us to go into the Mountains and make Friends with Nosu people was not good news to Kim and me. We had life wired, remember?

We talked about it incessantly. We prayed and fasted. Finally we agreed to stop talking about it, as it was messing up our happy Tolstoyian family life. But the next evening we went for a walk on the Idaho Falls greenbelt and talked about it all six miles.

We were willing.

Our goals were:

- Learn as much as possible about Nosu people.
- Communicate what we learned to our home church and others who were interested.
- Learn spoken Chinese well enough to explain the gospel.

I estimated that this would take three years, after which we would return to Idaho Falls.

Before our final decision, we talked with four sets of trustworthy friends who knew us well. They said things like:

"For most people this would be a bad idea, but I think it will work for you."

"Not only can I see you guys doing this, I can't see you not doing it."

"I'll be sorry to lose the time with you, but I support you."

"You fly, I'll hold the ropes."

Kim and I fasted and prayed another day and went for walks separately. We had a ceremonial secret ballot family vote, with two options, "stay" and "go". Anna was 7, Niels was 5, and we didn't tell them that their votes didn't really count. But "go" won by a 4-0 margin.

We had goodbye parties at church, at work, and with friends. Anna and Niels gave away most of their little kid toys, but packed away some favorite stuffed animals. They had a private going away party for them and put them in a storage box, right side up, with air holes.

Some asked us, "Don't you think it is risky to take kids to live in the Third World? There are nasty diseases and bad food and communists."

I never said it this succinctly, but I tried to answer back, "Don't you think it is risky to raise kids in the US? They could get addicted to computer games and get fat and lazy and feel superior and entitled."

We connected with Food for the Hungry International (FHI). They had a program that would allow us to get a visa to live in an area with some Nosu people. We'd need to raise $48,000 a year to join up. This was a bargain—the average overseas missionary at that time raised more than $75,000 per year. But we thought we could live on much less, so we started our own nonprofit, Mountain Friends, Inc., and subcontracted to FHI.

Our annual budget looked like this:

Round trip airfare for four	$5000
Food in US and China	$4000
Payroll tax	$4000
Tithe	$2400
Major medical health and evac insurance	$1500
US property tax and insurance	$1500
Rent in China	$1200
Local travel in China	$1000
Medical/dental	$800

Utilities	$500
Local travel in the US (gas)	$500
Homeschool supplies	$500
Clothes and outdoor gear	$500
Gifts	$500
Total (with $100 margin)	$24000

We lived on this budget for three years, then asked our board of directors for a raise, to account for a less favorable exchange rate.

Typically missionaries spend months in deputation, which is an archaic word for fund-raising. Their agency requires them to raise a certain amount for start-up expenses, typically about $30,000, and a percentage of their salary, before they can report for duty. We covered the start-up expenses out our of our savings and skipped the deputation period. I worked until a Friday and we left for China the next Monday. To save money on payroll fees, we arranged to be paid quarterly, and by the time our first paycheck was due, the $6,000 had come in to cover it.

Anna and Niels and Kim were great travelers. They liked airplane food and free in-seat movies and moving sidewalks and they didn't complain about time-zone changes. We didn't have anything shipped with us; we took only what we could carry within our baggage allowance. We were limited to 20 kg each in checked bags, and 5 kg in carry-ons. Half of the weight was a year's supply of homeschool books. Most of the other half was warm clothes and sleeping bags. We had 10 bags altogether, each with a name, like Big Green, Little Green, and the Blue Dragger, which had a broken wheel.

I provided a pep talk to the kids. "There is a time for horsing around, and a time to be serious. When we change planes or buses it is time to be serious. I need you to help me count the bags and not get separated." At each transfer we went into frenzied family action mode, identifying, stacking, and counting our 10 bags. We took five flights, a city bus, a long distance bus, and arrived in our new home[10] in China.

---

[10] We kept our house in Idaho and also referred to it as home. I often told the kids, "You should only marry one spouse and worship one God, but it is totally OK to have two places that you call home." We told them as we went back and forth from Idaho to China that they were like the Pevensie kids in the *Chronicles of Narnia,* occasionally getting transported from one world to another. The Pevensies moved by magic; we used Korean Air.

7 CHINESE PEOPLE

"Nothing and no one can destroy the Chinese people. They are relentless survivors." Pearl S. Buck

One of the many undervalued beauties of China is the ethnic mosaic. After we moved in and added English, the street we lived on in our new neighborhood had more native tongues than houses, by a score of seven to six. The native languages spoken by minorities were Tibetan, Nosu, Lisu, Miao, Bai, and Naxi.

The Nosu have a skin color inspired story to explain how some of the different people groups came into existence:

"When God was creating people, He prepared some special sticks and threw them into the fire. One stick jumped out and said, "It's too hot!" That stick was not quite done, and it became the father of the Han Chinese. Another stick was overdone, and it became the father of the Tibetans. The third stick was golden brown, just right, and it became the father of the Nosu."

Now every Chinese national carries an identification card, or *shenfenzheng*. Among other things, it identifies ethnicity. Ethnic statistics are easy to come by from the 2010 census, and I am using those numbers.

If most people speak of "a Chinese person" they are referring to Han Chinese people. This is fair as there are 1,220 million Han in China, about 92% of the total. But that still leaves 112 million people who are ethnic minorities, about the same number as the total population of France and the UK, combined.

Is it realistic to make generalizations about more than a billion people at once? No, but here goes. Han people are good at math, hardworking, like to drink tea and eat rice, have a religion which may blend Daoism, Buddhism and Confucianism[11], are hospitable to strangers, and are always up for a game of mahjong or a new business idea. Han people love boisterous dinner parties at restaurants that look like parking garages but serve food fit for an emperor.

I'm not in love with my generalization, but that first year Kim and I had lived in Chongqing, we had fallen in love with Han Chinese people and culture.

Tibetans are the best known Chinese minority. Even people who can't locate Tibet on a map can locate their bumper to put a 'Free Tibet' sticker on. There are about 6.3 million Tibetans in China.

While we lived in China, we employed two Tibetans as Chinese language tutors for our family, and Anna's best friend was a Tibetan girl. We had Tibetans in our house almost every day for six years and got to know several of them well. I read every book on Tibet I could find.

Tibetans are engaging, hospitable, fun-loving, attractive people. In the 1960s the CIA secretly brought 300 Tibetan men to Colorado to train for an invasion of Chinese Tibet[12]. Our military loved how they would jump out of airplanes without fear, like it was a game. When I hiked into a Tibetan village I would be met with open smiles and offers to come drink yak butter tea.

Tibetans have few equals in religious observance. I have seen hundreds of women circling a holy mountain by bowing face down, taking one step, prostrating again, one step, and so on for the circumnavigation.

Historically, two of the most important Lamas were the

---

[11] Unless they are Muslim or Christian or atheist.
[12] Ping-pong diplomacy prevailed, and the invasion never occurred.

Dalai and Panchan. Of course the Dalai Lama is an international celebrity, but when the Panchan Lama came through our town in 2006, he was able to draw a crowd. Forty thousand Tibetans streamed on foot to a grassland to watch him pass by in a Land Cruiser and give a blessing. I saw him through the open window, a bored and beatific teenager.

Tibet was a place of scenic misery before and after the Dalai Lama left in 1959, when the Chinese tanks rolled. In the 1950s one out of seven Tibetans was a slave. There was not a public school or a paved road or a modern hospital. Tibet was essentially a Buddhist theocracy, with the monks running the show. I don't claim to understand the deeper meanings in Tibetan Buddhism, but the way it appears in daily village life is not attractive. I have been to villages where everyone was skinny, except for the monks, who were fat. The poor farmers rarely asked me to give them money, but the richer monks often did, insistently, and became indignant when I refused. Ordinary Tibetans have told me in confidence, "Actually being part of China has made our lives better."

Many Tibetans live in traditional houses, which use post and beam infrastructure and rammed earth walls. In a village, the ground floor is used for animals, and the family accesses the second floor by a rickety wooden ladder. In locations where the quality of the rammed earth allows, a third floor is constructed. There is rarely indoor plumbing. Some have outhouses cantilevered off of the second floor living quarters. It is not prudent to walk underneath.

Tibetans love their dogs. Mastiffs look like lions and are spoiled like children. A good one will cost a year's pay. In one village we visited, old people remembered that in the insanity of the Cultural Revolution, the young Red Army thugs had everyone in town bring their dogs to the town square, and, as an object lesson in community demoralization, shot them.

Tibetans are one of a handful of cultures in the world that practice polyandry, in which a woman marries two husbands. Typically they are brothers, and all children are reckoned to the elder. The traditional local explanation for this practice is that men were often away on long journeys—for example on the Tea

Horse Road—and it allowed brothers to rotate between home and caravan, with one wife who remained to take care of the home and children.

Tibetans also occasionally practice polygamy. Once I was traveling with a mini-van driver, and we were sprawled in our simple hostel after dinner. He looked up from the game he was playing on his cell phone and asked me a getting-to-know-you question. "How many wives do you have?"

"Only one," I answered, "but it is OK; she is a good one."

He had two women that he referred to as wives, in different towns.

Now Tibet is managed by the Chinese government as a kind of grand scale Disneyland. Lamaseries are tourist attractions, and there are dances every night.

There are 55 recognized minority groups in China. Several are used as catch-alls for disparate groups that share at least one characteristic. The Yi minority has been described as the catch-all for "people groups who live in the mountains and celebrate the torch festival." There are about 8.7 million Yi. One of the biggest and most distinctive of the Yi subgroups is the Nosu[13]. There are about 2.5 million Nosu.

My family lived with a Nosu family for three years. We participated with them in weddings and funerals as family members. I have literally read every book and studied every scholarly article published on the Nosu in English. If I were playing Jeopardy and the Daily Double occurred in the Nosu category, I would bet everything.

The Nosu are clan based. There is no history of a centralized king or high priest. They often feud with other clans. During World War II, a Western military officer evaluated the Nosu as potential guerilla fighters against the Japanese, who were occupying China. His conclusion was essentially, "The Nosu have the potential to be some of the best guerrillas in the world.

---

[13] Nosu is the traditional Wade Giles Romanization. The modern pinyin is Nuosu. Both spellings are approximations of a round lipped "ooah" vowel that is not really used in English. I use Nosu instead of Nuosu in this book because it is smoother for English speakers to read. If you want to Google this people group, try "Nuosu Yi."

But I'm not sure we could rely on them to only kill the bad guys."

The Nosu were in open civil war against the Chinese as recently as the 1950s. They used to hold slaves and raid Chinese villages. One of my Chinese friends told me, "When I was little, the Nosu would come outside our village and howl like coyotes. We were scared to death, and the little kids would be hidden."

Another time we were on a road trip with a Nosu grandma and she struck up a conversation with an older guy at a service station. When we asked her who it was, she said, "Oh, he used to be my dad's slave."

The Nosu are xenophobic, which means they usually don't like outsiders. They rarely marry outside their ethnic group. When I hiked into a Nosu village I was met with women and kids ducking into houses and men suddenly trying to act busy to avoid eye contact.

The Nosu traditionally were semi-nomadic and practiced slash and burn agriculture. The term anthropologists use for this is swidden agriculturists. When the soil was depleted of nutrients they moved. Since they lived in forested areas they became skilled at building log cabins. The cabins were not intended as permanent homes and were constructed accordingly, quick and dirty.

Arranged marriages were and are the norm. The ideal match used to be between "cross-cousins," that is, two cousins who do not share the same family name. For example a man's daughter can marry his sister's son, but not his brother's son. When we left in 2010 this practice was in transition, as the older generation preferred it on the basis of tradition, and the younger generation was beginning to protest on the basis of genetics. Providing a son is a vital measure of performance for a wife. If no children or only girls come along, a mistress may be arranged.

The Nosu are animistic. They believe in an active spirit world with ghosts and demons. Once I was doing a Bible study with some Nosu and we came to Mark chapter 5, where Jesus exorcises demons and casts them into pigs. Nobody was thrown by that, and it started an avalanche of stories about demons, all told in a matter-of-fact way. "One time we had a guy in our village with a demon, and the bimo[14] got it out of him, and put it in a bottle, and we corked it and threw it in the ditch. I bet the guy who tried to recycle that bottle got a surprise!"

A Tibetan home with second story outhouse.

---

[14] A bimo is a Nosu shaman, a well-respected intermediary between the physical and spiritual world. He is often the only person in his village who can read the Nosu script.

8 THE HOOD

"You can impress people at a distance, you can only impact them up close." Howard Hendricks

Some of the other expat Christians in town placed a high value on "community." Their idea was that the locals would see us living together in harmony and be drawn to want that for themselves. They were happy to have our family move in at first, partly because they thought Kim would help with homeschooling everyone's kids and I would teach the kids to shoot a basketball. "Remember kids, BEEF: balance, elbow in, eyes on the rim, follow through." They also genuinely liked us and wanted to develop friendships.

We placed a high value on "identification." The idea was that if you lived as much like the local people as possible, it communicated respect to them and made it easier to introduce new ideas. We believed that if we were too close to the other expats it would interfere with identification.

The others placed a high value on "authenticity." The idea was the worst thing you could do was to pretend you didn't have problems. This seemed to me to result in a competition for who could have the most problems and complain about them in the most self-absorbed detail.

We placed a high value on not complaining even when life was hard. We expected our kids to work diligently and listen to us. We were seen as goody-goody, or even worse, not authentic.

The clash of values made conflict inevitable, and we had a rocky relationship with the expat community. Most of the fault was ours. I found it much harder to show grace to American Christians than to Chinese animists. The values I resented, community and authenticity, are good values, even foundational to the Christian faith. Living overseas with other expats always seemed to intensify relationships and magnify differences, and I had over-reacted.

Consistent with our value of identification, we lived in an ordinary neighborhood—the kind that schoolteachers, bus drivers, and policemen lived in. Our house had five bedrooms, an outhouse with Eastern toilet, a well for drawing water, and a kitchen with a woodstove. The kitchen was the only room in the house with heat of any kind. There was not a shower, or even a sink. We took baths near the woodstove in a big basin, with a sheet strung up for privacy.

We tried to eat a local diet, mostly potatoes, rice, and stir fry. After six weeks Anna and I splurged and shared a can of Coca Cola, and the sugar and caffeine went straight to my head harder than any alcohol.

Anna and Niels still played with the foreign kids on Sundays, but the rest of the week they hung with the locals. All of the kids came to our house at first, while we were a novelty. Some mean little girls stole Anna's favorite stuffed animals, but some nice little girls brought her snacks and talked about their pets. Niels played soccer and toy guns. These kids spoke a variety of ethnic languages at home, but at school and in the neighborhood, Chinese was the *lingua franca*. Anna's and Niels' language ability improved quickly.

A young Chinese pastor, married to an American, stayed with us and said, "Considering language study, lifestyle, and family, you guys are doing better than any other Westerners I have ever seen in China."

His wife added, "In our job we see Westerners all the time in many different cities, and he has never said anything like this before. It is a genuinely high compliment.[15]"

Kim and I worked hard on language study and wrote the curriculum for a two-week English camp. All four of us traveled by second class long distance bus to the other cities where there were outreaches to Nosu people.

The expectation of personal space varies from culture to culture, and this is evident on public busses. On one trip, a grandmother thanked me for coming to China and showed her appreciation by holding my hand for a couple of hours. Another time a young mother in the seat next to me pulled the hem of her T-shirt up to her neck and fed her baby. A different young woman, carsick, turned to me, smiled, and threw up in my lap. My family and I became imperturbable travelers, and events like this did not bother us at all.

Back at home, Little Bird helped us with our Chinese, cooked on weekday evenings and ate dinner with us, sometimes with other friends. During and after dinner we liked to tell stories.

Little Bird began, "You know about my brother falling off the electric pole and breaking his back, right? What I didn't tell you was that it was caused by a snake. When my brother was healthy, he was driving truck. One day he saw a snake by the side of the road, killed it, had it in a soup, and forgot about it. Later, after he fell, our family had the bimo come and do a ceremony to find out what sin had caused the accident. He sprinkled the blood of a sacrificed chicken and examined the chicken bones to divine what the sin was. Then he said that since my brother was born in the year of the snake, he shouldn't ever kill one. My brother remembered eating the snake and told the bimo about it. He told my brother that if he didn't ever kill any more animals, that sin would be forgiven. He hasn't killed a snake since, and he also hasn't killed any other wild animals."

One of our language tutors, a 20-year-old Tibetan girl, continued, "That reminds me of a snake story. When I was young, my grandfather lived with us. My mother liked my older sister best, my father liked my younger sister best, but my

---

[15] Having a bad day, I could take this compliment out of my back pocket, dust it off, shine it up, and be good to go for another week.

grandfather liked me best. He always cleaned the house. I liked him so much I would go get a broom and sweep with him without being asked. One of my chores was to feed the pigs. During the summer there were sometimes big snakes near the pigpen.

"My grandfather would say, 'It's too dangerous for *you* to feed the pigs. I'll send your little sister instead.' "

Another one of our tutors said, "That reminds me of when I was little. When I was five years old, I used to play at swimming in a big water tank. I couldn't swim, so I used an old tire to stay afloat. One day I took my three-year-old brother. He couldn't swim either. My mom caught us. She was holding a stick, but couldn't reach me in the middle of the tank."

"She commanded, 'Come out of there!'"

"I responded, 'I will if you won't spank me with that stick!'"

"She agreed, but when I came out, she used it to spank me anyway. I was angry at her for a long time."

Her mother happened to be there, and she added, laughing, "What was really funny was while I was spanking you, your little brother came out of the tank with no clothes on. He ran about a mile naked through the village to get his grandmother to save him from getting his spanking."

I said, "My story doesn't involve snakes or nudity, but we know an attractive young female Chinese friend who owns her own home. Two weeks ago a high ranking Tibetan Living Buddha (a person who has achieved enlightenment prior to his reincarnation) came to her house. He said that house would be an auspicious site to build a shrine. So could he buy it? Never mind the cost. The next day they were discussing the details and talking about a price of $50,000, far more than she paid for it, when he mentioned one other detail. Part of the bargain was that she needed to marry his little brother. Sure, the youngster used to have a drinking problem, but he was reforming nicely. She said 'no deal' and the Living Buddha went back to Lhasa. Reportedly, his little brother wept bitterly."

Later, Kim and I discussed Living Buddhas. Since they have achieved enlightenment, they no longer need to practice self-denial or follow religious rules. Unlike normal monks in the monastery, Living Buddhas can sleep with whomever, drink alcohol, and eat meat with no cosmic backlash. We thought that some Christians rationalize a similar approach to being immune from following normal rules. "Since I…(pick one: gave up everything to move to China, adopted kids from the Third World, am a gifted speaker, am a gifted musician, am nicer than anyone you've ever met)…ordinary expectations should not apply to me. I don't need to…(pick one: work a full day, account for my spending, speak graciously, be faithful to my spouse, treat my friends with humility.)" We decided that we would try our best to be ordinary pilgrims, and not act like Living Buddhas.

I suspect the locals paid scant attention to the value systems of the expats. They had more pragmatic ways of referring to all of the foreign families. One was "the family with five kids." Another was "the family with boys that look like girls." We were "the family whose kids speak Chinese." I was sinfully proud of how well Anna and Niels were able to fit in, and remain proud today. But I'm admitting the sin, which shows that at the very least, I am authentic.

This is not our house.

9 CHINESE TEARS

"Sometimes I think of Abraham, how one star he saw had been lit for me. He was a stranger in this land, and I am that, no less than he." Rich Mullins, Sometimes by Step

We didn't ever learn Tibetan or Nosu. We learned Chinese.

When someone is describing learning Chinese they will describe a character like 泪(*lei*). "See the rectangles on the right? Those represent eyes. See the line with the dots on the left? That represents water. Eyes with water are tears. *Lei* is used in words for tears. Isn't that simply beautiful?"

What they don't mention is you need a few thousand characters to read a newspaper or a novel, and only a few of them are beautiful and easy like 泪. Most have combinations of components in which the meanings are obscured by antiquity. They are learned mostly by memorization. In your forties, it is hard to memorize anything, but we gave it our best shot. Once I was working through flash cards with my tutor and we flipped up 舞. I had no idea which character it was and sighed, "Wooh, that's a hard one."

My tutor clapped her hands happily and said, "You're right, its *wu*!"

But memorizing characters is only part of the challenge in learning Chinese. For many adult English speakers, learning to use tones correctly is even more terrorizing.

Chinese has four tones: first-high, second-rising, third-dipping, and fourth-falling. In Roman characters the tones can be indicated with diacritical marks over the vowels. Consider the characters that are pronounced "pu", as in Winnie the Pu. The dictionary I am using has 37 of them and each character uses one of the four tones. For example: 痡, first tone pū; 葡, second tone pú; 朴, third tone pǔ; and 瀑, fourth tone pù. Our first tutor had us practice the tones by saying quite loudly, "pū-pú-pǔ-pù! pū-pú-pǔ-pù!" Sometimes, childishly, I would smile and think, "I'm saying pu-pu!"

We found it was best to change tutors every few months, as they adapted to our language skills and changed their vocabulary and grammar to a special variety we could understand better. New tutors were more representative of standard speaking. But language learning is perfect for developing friendships, and some of our old tutors still dropped by for meals and outings.

Anna and Niels disliked having tutors at first, then became grateful their new-found language ability had opened their circle of potential friends from a few foreigners to everyone.

We all committed language *faux pas*. I went into a small shop looking for toilet paper, and asked the shop girl for a "toilet pig."

Kim went to a neighbor's house, smiled, and said, "Your son is definitely *not* invited to my son's birthday party," and left.

I tried to ask a young married lady if she wanted to have kids someday, like I do, and what came out was, "Do you want to have kids, with me?"

She laughed and replied, "I suggest you talk to your wife first."

When I started learning how to read and write, my biggest felt need was to be able to order from a menu. So I offered to provide an English language translation at several of our favorite restaurants. Here is an excerpt from one, with the prices in the Chinese currency, Yuan. The exchange rate then was about Y8 to $1.

鱼香肉丝	Fish tasting pork	Y14
莲藕	Lotus root	Y6
小瓜	Zucchini	Y6

宫爆鸡丁	Kung pao chicken	Y35
糖醋排骨	Sweet & sour pork ribs	Y18
苦瓜	Bitter squash[16]	Y6
竹荪汤	Bamboo shoot soup	Y20

Sometimes when I studied Chinese in the afternoon I would listen to dialogues or stories on my MP3 player. I noticed concentrating on the Chinese would immediately put me to sleep—apparently a defense mechanism, like someone undergoing torture who passes out from extreme pain. This gave me a great idea that changed my life.

I had always had trouble going back to sleep if I woke up at, say, 2 AM. It was worse in China because the street noise and high elevation made sleeping difficult at any time. I started taking an MP3 player to bed and listening to stories in Chinese to put myself back to sleep. It worked! I had a set of 40 dramatized Bible stories that I listened to repeatedly. The voice actor who portrayed Satan would hiss like a snake. Sometimes I would already be asleep and the Chinese Satan would enter my dreams[17], and I would wake up, disoriented and afraid. But no problem, I could stick in the earbuds, dial up Deuteronomy, and be back asleep before the Shema was finished.

Chinese is a difficult language for Westerners to learn. Most are wildly overconfident and say they are "fluent" as soon as they can buy bananas in the market. One American mother told us her six-year-old was getting so good at Chinese she made him stop using it, afraid it would damage his English. I spent some time with her kid and by my estimate he knew less than 10 words.

The US Foreign Service has a more objective rating system than that over-protective mom. Using their data, on a 0-5 level of proficiency, after 2000 hours of use, an average American learning an easier language, like Spanish, would be at a level 3. In Chinese, they would be at a 1+. This brings many to tears.

---

[16] Everything on this menu was delicious, except for bitter squash. Inserting it here just gave me a convulsive twitch.

[17] I always understood every word when I dreamt. My Chinese was great, in my dreams.

Fortunately there is a beautiful Chinese word for tears, which we already knew.

We began to make friends when our Chinese level was 0-. We needed friends who had a sense of humor, like Diji.

10 DIJI

"Kindred spirits are not so scarce as I used to think. It's splendid to find out that there are so many of them in the world." L. M. Montgomery, Anne of Green Gables

Sometimes nine-year-old Anna was lonely. We prayed God would send her a best friend—someone with whom she could have sleepovers and dress up long-suffering pets like our dog, Rontu. When we prayed we were imagining an American girl, maybe like her best friends back in Idaho. God has a better imagination, and he sent her the Tibetan Anne Shirley.

Ten-year-old Diji was tall, pretty, and also lonely. Her dad drank too much and her parents argued loudly. She came to our house almost every day after school the next three years. She would run into our kitchen, slide across the floor, point at her face, and ask, "Do you think I'm even cuter than I was yesterday?" or, "They talked about having a beauty contest at school, but the teachers looked at me and said, 'What's the point? We all know Diji would win.' "

The first time I met her I was playing soccer with the neighborhood kids in the alley. After we finished the match[18], she approached me like we were old friends and described every

---

[18] It was never like we'd just play to 7 and be done. The reasons we would finish were: we'd lose the ball in the sewer, or over a fence with a mean dog, the ball would pop, or I would sprain something.

kid in sight. "You see that girl, the fat one? She is really good at math. That boy with the red shirt has a brother who is a monk in the monastery. You know Ah Ling Ling, right? I saw her playing with one of Anna's stuffed animals…" And on she went for 20 minutes, not worried that I only understood half of what she was saying.

She and Anna became inseparable. When they had sleepovers they would chatter in Chinese for hours. They went shopping and bought cheap nasty Chinese candy and dressed up their pets. They promised to come to each other's weddings.

Diji's dad was a local chief of police. He was 6'4" and in his younger days had been an all-province basketball player. He came to our house to play ping pong. I am no dummy when it comes to policemen, and he won at ping pong more than our skill levels would have predicted. Their family invited us for holidays and we talked about whether we should arrange a marriage between Diji and Niels[19].

Diji's mom, also a tall, attractive Tibetan, was a wonderful cook. At one of the festival meals she made 12 different meat dishes for one dinner. She could never get over the fact our Chinese was not perfect, and she continued to use really loud baby talk with us, even after years had gone by and it wasn't necessary.

Tibetan style houses have rammed earth walls with grass on top to prevent erosion. In the winter the grass dies. Once at Chinese New Year, Diji, Anna, and Niels were playing with sparklers. One of them—still not clear to me which one—accidentally threw a sparkler into the neighbor's courtyard and started their grass wall on fire. Flames were a couple feet high and in danger of spreading to the shake roof on the wooden house when we got buckets of water in place to put it out. My most vivid memory of the event is the expression on Diji's face when the fire was at its peak. Her eyes were like half-dollars.

Long after the fire, in a reflective mood, she asked Kim and me, "Do you think I'm hyperactive?"

---

[19] In this culture of arranged marriages, people often joke about it when their kids are small. You know it is no longer a joke when money changes hands, or a pig gets killed.

Kim replied, "No, you behave really well. Who says you're hyperactive?"

She replied, "My mother. My father. My big sister. All of my teachers. My aunt. My grandmother. Actually, everybody I know."

Anna and Diji.

11 ZEYI

Calvin: "Look! A trickle of water running through some dirt. I'd say our afternoon just got booked solid." Bill Watterson, The Complete Calvin and Hobbes

After Anna and Diji became close, we thought we'd try our luck again and prayed for a friend for Niels. Once again God came through and sent Niels his Nosu twin, Zeyi.

Before he came to live with us, Zeyi lived in a flea-poor village at 11,000 feet with a single mom and two little brothers.

Here is how Zeyi's dad died, as told by his aunt.

"Jiefu wasn't an ordinary Nosu man. He was tall and handsome. The day he came to take my sister away to live with him, everyone in the village thought he was the most handsome man they had ever seen. And he was not an ordinary father. He really loved his boys, and, unlike most men here, he played with them all the time. The two older boys were always climbing on him and riding on his back, just like Niels does with you. He treated my sister great; he never said a harsh word to her. Everything he did, he did well. He built this house by himself, in just a few weeks."

"He worked at the copper mine on the mountain behind us. He was a crew leader. One day as the day shift was coming out, they said 'It's really dangerous in there; there is going to be a collapse soon.' Jiefu told them to hurry and get out and told his crew not to go in. He looked at the problem and saw a way to fix it. He told some men to lower him down on a rope and pull him back up when he was done. He fixed the main problem, but, as he was doing it, a rock from higher up dislodged and fell on him, crushing his chest. By the time the other men got him to the mine entrance he was dead.

"Some workers came to this house that we are in right now and told my sister. At first she didn't believe them. She thought they must have mistaken someone else's body for his. Then she realized it was true.

"Nosu men can't be buried in their regular clothes, it interferes with their spirit's journey to heaven. Jiefu was still a young man, so his special burial clothes hadn't been made yet. My sister immediately started sewing. She sewed as fast as she could, and heaven must have helped her, because she finished in two hours. Then she started off to the copper mine.

"Can you imagine my sister, six-year-old Zeyi holding one hand, his four-year-old brother holding her other, a six-month-old baby strapped to her back, a bundle of funeral clothes under her arm, climbing that mountain in the dark to go see her dead husband?

"When they arrived at the mine the men led them to the body. Even though Jiefu had been dead several hours, when his wife and children came up to him, a drop of blood came out of his nose, and a tear came out of his eye. And when his oldest son came to give him a bite of rice, to give his spirit strength for his journey, people said his mouth opened.

"Everyone at the mine was crying and very emotional, except my sister. She just told her children, 'Your father is going away now and won't be coming back.' She didn't cry and even now when the children or our mother are around she acts strong. But sometimes when we are alone together, she cries."

After we spent a weekend with their family one of the little boys started to call me Daddy, and the others told him to knock it off.

The first time Zeyi came from the village to our house in town he played soccer with Niels, then came in. We thought our house was simple and modest. We had everyone sit down for dinner, and Zeyi sat right on top of the table. We told him to sit on one of the benches, and we would put the food on the table. Later one of his cousins was teasing him about it and he said, "How was I supposed to know where to sit? They have so much stuff it seemed like a furniture store!"

In stark contrast to most American and Chinese boys at the time, neither Niels nor Zeyi owned or cared about computers or video games. When they had time together after school—which was basically every day for three years—they played basketball and soccer, shot slingshots, went fishing with nets, and ran around the grasslands with Rontu and the other dogs. They had a real boyhood with frequent infusions of exertion, abrasions, and natural vitamin D—not daily injections of electronic daydreams from a flickering screen.

I played them one-on-two basketball hundreds of times. I always tried to help Zeyi's English by keeping score. "Three to two, four to two, five to two, I win!" He was a sneaky, lightning-fast guard who cared even less about English than video games. He never learned to count past three.

Niels and Zeyi were the same age, same smallish size for their age, same haircut, same interests. When they would run around together people called them "The Twins." "Look, a little foreign kid and a little Nosu kid. They are like twins; isn't that weird!" They were both minorities from the Han and Tibetan perspective, both mocked for it, and it made them even closer.

For years I functioned as Zeyi's father figure. I made him be nice to his cousins, keep his elbow in on his jump shot, and questioned his fashion sense. I would carry him around the yard under my arm so I could give him a hug without embarrassing him. I went to his school events and cheered for him on Parent's Day. One of his grade school teachers said to me, "It is so odd Zeyi is close with your family but has such bad English. He is even worse than the others students! But frankly, he is the best in the whole school at basketball."

The twins.

12 AHMA

"Strong women only marry weak men." Bette Davis

When we met Ahma, Little Bird's mother, she was selling pitchwood and we stopped to buy some. She gave Anna and Niels each a cookie and they said, "Thank you," and ate them. Later Ahma told us she often tried to give cookies to other foreign kids, they thought her hands were too dirty and wouldn't take one.

Ahma was a story teller. "When I was a little girl, we had a big family. My father had three wives and about 60 slaves. I remember one day a man came to our village with two little girls about my age, and my father bought them for 20 pieces of silver. Not long after that the laws changed and slavery became illegal. The government freed the slaves and gave them all of my family's property. We had nothing. This was during the Cultural Revolution and all kinds of crazy things happened. My mother was forced to cut her long braids and burn her traditional clothes. I told her, 'You're not my mother, you look like a man! Get away from me!' (a pause, with tears) There were criticism meetings where my parents sat in the front with dunce caps on and people insulted them. My mother died from the stress, and I had to start taking care of my little brothers and sisters. I was nine years old...

"My husband was one of the first people in this county who learned to drive, and he made good money. He was a good man until he started drinking too much. Then he started living with another woman at the other end of his truck route. He threatened my four kids and me with a gun. Finally we had to run away. The kids were starting to yell at him when he hit me, and I was afraid he would kill one of them. It was winter but we walked 100 kilometers to a different village to get away from him. We stepped in each other's tracks in the snow so there would only be one set of footprints, and we would be harder to follow...

"The village I lived in after I left my husband was up high in the mountains, about 11,000 feet. It was really remote, and there were lots of wild animals, like wolves, mountain sheep, bear, and deer. Once we went even further into the hills to pick wild plants for medicine to sell, and we came across the tracks of a tiger. His prints were as big as a horse's hoof, only with claws. We didn't have a gun with us and we were terrified. Then that night we heard him roar. First he went like this: "arrrr." Then later he went like this: "rrraaarr." The bimo back in the village said that meant someone would die. Sure enough, six months later, one of my older brothers died. The bimo said from the time the tiger roared, he had already eaten my brother's soul. You know that one girl your company gave a scholarship to, the one who lost her father when she was little? That was her dad...

"Remember when Little Bird started coming to your house to cook? No one told you guys, but there was a big argument in our family. Some people thought you would take her away and sell her into slavery. But I thought you were good people, and I spoke in favor of letting her work at your house. But then after about a year, you bought her an airplane ticket to fly with you to Kunming for a conference so she could watch Anna and Niels. At that time, several people said, 'Aha! I told you so! Once they get her to the city they will sell her to the other foreigners! You've seen the last of your daughter!' When you all came back they were surprised."

Ahma could recite her genealogy for more than 20 generations. Illiterate, she had it memorized on her knuckles, and touched her hand with each name. When we traveled with her and she met another Nosu, they would compare ancestry to help decide what level of responsibility they had for hosting each other. If the relationship was close enough, even if no one had met before, we all got invited to dinner, and an unlucky goat or pig went in the pot.

Ahma had a life of poverty and tragedy and she loved to laugh. Once she told us about a lady friend of hers who accidentally went into the men's side of the village outhouse. A man came in and started to leave in embarrassment. "Come on in if you want," the lady said, "at my age there's nothing I haven't seen before!" Ahma loved that story and she would tell it over and over, throwing her hands up and head back, laughing harder each time.

Her life story seemed to have more in common with the book of Genesis than the 21st century. She had seen arranged polygamy, slaves, ritual curses, divinations, relational trickery, hospitality to ensure safety, herd size as wealth, clan based society, tribal feuds, and invading armies. If Jacob, Esau, and Rachel had lived 3000 years later and spoke the language, they would have felt right at home with the Nosu.

Ahma loved Anna and Niels. Sometimes, straight-faced, she would introduce them to people who didn't know us as her own grandchildren. You could see the wheels turning: "How could that be, with blue eyes and blond hair? Are they some kind of albino?" But before they had a chance to ask, Ahma would have started on another story.

Ahma and her sisters.

13 LANDLORDS

"I think daily life is the most beautiful and wonderful thing anyone can have." Ana Tijoux

At an elevation of 10,000 feet, the air pressure is about 69% of the pressure at sea level. Even though the percentage of oxygen in the atmosphere remains the same as at sea level, the air is less dense, and each breath takes in less oxygen for the body to use. The human body eventually adapts to the decrease in oxygen, and Tibetans are some of the best adapted humans. Even so, they believe it is better for their elderly to move to lower elevation to reduce their altitude-related health risks.

One of Ahma's best friends, a Tibetan widow about 70 years old, fit in this category. Her family influenced her to sell her home and move to Kunming. She was attached to her ramshackle one-acre property, with its houses, pigpens, gardens, and memories, and she did not want to sell to strangers, so she offered it to Ahma for $6,000, far below market value.

Ahma had a problem: cash flow. She probably did not have $60, and, understandably, there was no chance any bank would give a home loan to an illiterate widow with no steady job. Of course she polled her extended family to see how much money could be raised, but it was not nearly enough.

Capitalists to the rescue! I withdrew $6,000 worth of Chinese money from the ATM and arranged to rent one of the houses on the property for 10 years, at $600 per year, which would give her enough to buy the house. We wrote up a rental contract, and Little Bird and Ahma used the money to close the deal. Little Bird, with her 6th grade education and business sense, read the purchase contract and co-signed on the deed. By now her first child, Lydia, had come along, and she was very motivated to move out of their tiny rented shack.

Three things happened. Ahma and her family suddenly went from looking for bottles to recycle to being landowners. My family had rented a house we liked, for half the normal cost. And all of us now lived together on the same property.

Life together on a winter day might have gone like this:

0700 – Ahma got up and built a fire in her house. I got up and built a fire in our house. Little Bird and her husband pushed a cart to some small restaurants to pick up scraps that had been saved for them. They boiled the scraps and fed the 12 pigs. I worked on a community development project idea, using Wenlin software on my laptop to help with translation, feet by the fire.

0800 – Kim, Niels, Anna, Zeyi, and Lydia all got up to have breakfast. Zeyi left for school; and after finishing our family Bible study over pancakes, Anna and Niels started homeschool.

0900 – Kim did the laundry. The tiny plastic washing machine was frozen, so we had to carry it to a sunny part of the courtyard and let it thaw before she could start. The water pipes were also frozen, so she had to break the ice and dip water from a cistern for each cycle of several loads. I kept a fire in the wood stove, and Kim came in periodically to warm her chapped red hands, and work on curriculum for the next English camp.

1000 – Little Bird and Ahma began to split pitchwood to put into small bundles that could be sold in the market. I helped them split the wood and as we worked, we talked[20]. The air temperature was below freezing and the shady parts of the courtyard had snowdrifts, but warm in the high altitude sun, we took off our wool jackets.

Little Bird's husband helped for a short time, then went back

---

[20] Many of the stories in this book were told as we split pitchwood in the courtyard.

inside to take a nap. Usually Little Bird and her husband spoke to each other in Nosu, but sometimes they would use Chinese if they wanted me to be in on the conversation. Little Bird wanted me to understand what she said to her husband now, loudly, "You lazy pile of dog poop, why don't you stay out here and help us work?" There was no answer from inside.

1300 – After lunch, our Chinese tutors arrived, and Kim, Anna, Niels, and I practiced vocabulary and pronunciation for an hour.

1400 – Niels and I played basketball. I reminded him to dribble with his left hand just as much as he dribbled with his right hand, and to never look at the ball, always keep your eyes up.

1500 – Zeyi returned from school, threw his homework disdainfully on his unmade bed, yelled for Niels, and they went tearing up the hill for some tomfoolery. Anna noticed one of Little Bird's four dogs seemed to be sick, so she got out the de-worming medicine and went to work. Kim and I went for a walk on the grassland. We saw ruddy ducks, griffon vultures, black necked cranes, and a Tibetan guy herding some sheep, using a dirt bike.

1600 – Little Bird and Lydia came over to our living room and Kim taught Lydia a few English words, while Little Bird laughed. I chopped firewood with the help of one of Little Bird's cousins, who was in town to buy medicine. Every couple of months a relative would drop off a truckload of wood from the village, but it had to be split and cut to length to fit inside our stove, so we processed firewood almost every day. We didn't have a chainsaw or splitter, so all of the work was done by hand.

1800 – To celebrate the cousin's visit, everyone in our family and Little Bird's family went out to eat spicy hot pot together. It was frosty cold and steam rolled off the boiling pots. We sat on tiny wooden stools, like you might find in a 19th century kindergarten, and ladled chicken, noodles, and broth into our bowls. We lingered at the restaurant for a couple of hours, because the food was savory, the conversation was sweet, and it would be a bitterly cold walk home.

2000 – When our family got to our house the fire was out, and we stamped our feet to stay warm until the living room heated. Since only one room in the house had any heat, which was the wood stove, the four of us radiated around it through the winter, like petals on a flower. As we thawed, I made popcorn, Kim sliced apples, and we read aloud from the Chronicles of Narnia.

2100 – The giant copper teakettle was boiling. We filled four one-liter Nalgene bottles to warm up our beds, gave each other hugs, and said good night.

In the courtyard on a snowy day.

14 THE NOSU RENASSAINCE MAN

"Give me neither poverty nor riches! Give me just enough to satisfy my needs. For if I grow rich I may say, 'Who is the Lord?' And if I am poor, I may steal and thus insult God's holy name."
Agur, Proverbs 30:8-9

"If you want to hike to that peak across the canyon from here, just get on the north ridge and follow that up to the summit. The elevation at the summit is just over 4000 meters. The wooded section has red panda, foxes, several kinds of pheasants, and grouse. There are musk deer around tree line. Of course there used to be way more animals when I was young, but development has pushed them back. The forest used to have China firs that took two men stretching their arms to reach around. Those are mostly gone now, too. It is nice to have roads and schools, but I miss the trees and animals. I found some bleached out horns from a mountain sheep once. Do you want to see them?"

We were talking in Chinese, but Teacher Lu, the Nosu Renaissance Man, was speaking my language.

He was rail thin with angular features, long arms, and big eyes. We were about the same age and some said we looked alike, which both of us took as a mild insult.

He had grown up in the mountains but was not provincial. After learning to read the Nosu script he had traveled to

Sichuan several times to study and access the old books, like Gandalf using Denethor's library in *The Lord of the Rings*.

He told me about how the Nosu had migrated down from what is now Sichuan province, in the area around SongPan, probably 2000 years ago, and how they had continued to move, clan by clan, to this day. He talked about Zhygge Alur, the Nosu hero, who may have consolidated some tribal groups into an army like Genghis Khan did with the Mongols, or maybe he was purely a myth, nobody knows for sure. Teacher Lu told me some scholars believe Chinese characters evolved from the Nosu script.

Like most village school teachers, he didn't make enough money to support a family, so he also had a subsistence farm with a bull for plowing, goats for grazing, buckwheat for frybread, and potatoes for storing through the winter.

When he wasn't teaching or farming he was combing the mountains for wild mushrooms and medicinal plants to harvest and sell. He knew the names and uses of everything in the forest. He was also a rare Nosu, a non-bimo who could read and write his own language.

The Nosu script is similar to Chinese—pictographic and ancient. It was probably used as far back as the Tang dynasty 1200 years ago, and an inscription on a bronze bell has been dated at 1485 AD. An educated Chinese person will know perhaps 8000 Chinese characters, but there are only about 800 Nosu characters in the syllabary. A Nosu adult can learn to read in a few weeks, and Teacher Lu taught many of his family members and friends in his free time. On one visit I slipped him an early copy of the Nosu Good Book and he read it, keeping it hidden when not in use.

Many Nosu men in the villages become alcoholics and it is difficult to have an interesting conversation with them. After a bottle, they begin to rant about the injustices of life, in an aggrieved tone like Huck Finn's dad. "Guvment? You call this a guvment?"[21]

Teacher Lu and I talked about trees, antlers, Nosu history,

---

[21] To be fair to the Nosu men, I could have written "Many Idaho men...", and left the rest of the paragraph unchanged.

the symbolism of the Torch Festival, parenting, literacy, and the New Testament.

If he had grown up and lived in a developed country, he would have been a college professor, a lawyer, or maybe even an electrical engineer. He would have automatic garage door openers, an SUV that gets good mileage, and a road bike with a carbon fiber frame.

Many people will say, "But he is happier in that simple scenic village without all the modern stuff." But actually it is not happier to be poor. He was missing a couple of teeth and it was too expensive to get them fixed. If he and his wife both got sick at the same time, they needed to decide who went to see a doctor and who stayed home to work in the fields.

Kim and I kind of pretended to be poor for several years in China. We wore the same clothes most days, didn't own a car, didn't have a sit down toilet or a shower. Really the poverty was a sham. We owned a home in the US, had money in a savings account, money in a 401k, money in a 403b. If we had gotten really sick or badly injured, our health insurance had a provision for evacuation to a country with good hospitals, like Thailand. We always had a margin and a plan B, and people in actual poverty do not have either.

My family always tries to live a life of voluntary simplicity and grateful minimalism. This may look a little like living poor, but it is the opposite. We grow strawberries for gourmet desserts and vegetables because they taste better than the ones in the store. Poor people grow the same reliable staples every year because they can't afford to risk a crop failure. Buckwheat and potatoes are not served in Michelin rated restaurants.

Poverty almost never happens for a single reason. Conservatives tend to blame poor people for their lack of work ethic; liberals tend to blame someone else for being oppressive. Both could be true at the same time and there could be other factors present as well, like bad weather or a bad flu season. Poor sanitation leads to many being perpetually sick and working at reduced capacity, which looks like laziness. Many are also perpetually lazy, which looks like a disease. Poverty is complicated. Even Jesus said that the poor will always be with us. But poverty is an evil to fight against, not a secret benefit to idealize.

Teacher Lu was my best local friend. It would have been great to travel with him to the Alps or backpack through Yellowstone Park and talk about the books we were reading; but he couldn't afford the airfare or get a travel visa, and he was always too busy with the potatoes.

A statue of the legendary Nosu hero Zhygge Alur.

15 EXPAT LIFE

"The best argument for Christianity is Christians: their joy, their certainty, their completeness. But the strongest argument against Christianity is also Christians—when they are somber and joyless, when they are self-righteous and smug in complacent consecration, when they are narrow and repressive, then Christianity dies a thousand deaths." Sheldon Van Auken, A Severe Mercy

The ultimate American expat experience was watching the Super Bowl while drinking good coffee.

A sneaky Singaporean had rigged an illegal descrambler to his TV so that he could get a broadcast from the Philippines, and he invited all of the foreigners to his house for a 7 AM Super Bowl breakfast party.

There were about 50 of us—missionaries, teachers, bar owners, bums, and businessmen. Good coffee was hard to come by in those days, and we drank it like a sacrament.

Eli Manning escaped the rush, David Tyree made the Helmet Catch, and Bill Belichick's Evil Empire was defeated. A crowded house full of people who didn't know each other forgot about China for three hours and celebrated the best American football game of all time, which still (probably) had no eternal cosmic significance.

Relationships between expats in China were not always filled with this level of harmonious sacramental joy.

Some missionaries were not trustworthy financially. We learned this first hand as our renters missed 18 consecutive monthly payments, even as they spent money freely on other priorities. When I showed their leader their contract, he glanced at it, pushed it aside, and said "I don't really care about contracts. I care about ministry."

Others did not appear to be trustworthy in their use of alcohol and their personal conduct. There were homes where we would not let Anna and Niels have sleepovers. We felt that sometimes our children were safer around the local animists than the expat Christians. By God's kindness they were not harmed by either.

After a year around the missionaries, Kim had a faith crisis. She said, "Some of these people don't believe what they are saying, they have just found an easy way to make money. What if the apostles were also faking it and we have a fake Bible? I'm not sure I believe any of this anymore."

I countered, "What is your alternative? Christianity looks better when it is compared with its alternatives. And 11 or so of the apostles believed it enough to die for it. If people here started getting crucified or burned at the stake, the fakes would shut up and clear out pretty fast."

On our next visit to Idaho Kim mentioned the faith crisis to a couple of older ladies at church, who didn't seem to believe her. How could someone who was a good enough Christian to move to China doubt their own faith? "Just pray about it, sweetie, and I'm sure you'll feel better tomorrow."

Life among the expats wasn't all bad. We met some kindred spirits and became lifelong friends. Among them were brilliant, hardworking linguists who lived in a Tibetan village in a huge old house and spent more each month on coffee than rent. We talked about books, hiked, and laughed.

And sometimes having an expat community to go to for help was a game changer. Once I was visiting a village school when a Nosu man introduced himself and said, "I heard you are a friend of the Nosu people. I have walked 10 miles to find you. Could you come and help my son?"

His handsome, athletic, long haired 20-year-old had been a good student and responsible kid, but he had gotten so unpredictable and violent he had to be locked in a pig pen. The boy had been confined for weeks, and his hands had sores on them from trying to beat his way out.

The pig pen roof was too low for him to stand up and I also had to crouch when they unlocked the door for me. I said something banal like, "Hi, how's it going?"

He smiled at me, muttered something, spit in my face, and came at me. His dad and some others held him back as he screamed, and they locked the door from the outside as the boy beat on it from the inside. I was no help; I was out of my league on many levels.

I called a friend, an American doctor who spoke perfect Chinese, and explained the situation. He said, "It sounds like schizophrenia, or maybe demon possession. I'll go take a look." He drove to the village the next day and took along some medicine, which worked. The people in the village thought he had done a miracle. I agreed.

Later, I showed a picture of the 20-year-old to our Chinese language tutors, who were both 20 years old themselves, as well as being girls. They both had the same reaction and said: "Wow, the crazy guy is hot!"

Another Singaporean expat had a gift for reconciliation. He helped heal a rift between two local groups and brought encouragement and maturity wherever he went. Once I gave his ministry a cash donation and said, "The good you do here more than makes up for the harm the rest of us do."

As an engineer, I love to quantify, so I finally developed A Field Guide to Missionaries.

5 % – Legitimate heroes. They have good non-fiction books written about them. The doctor I mentioned will have one written about him someday.

5% – Outright fakes. They promise little kids in a village candy if they will pose in front of their Vacation Bible School sign for a photo, which they will then use in a fundraising newsletter. They don't actually do a VBS, and they don't even give the kids their candy. They write fictional books, with themselves as the hero.

5% – Not fakes but really lazy. They have realized supporters and agencies don't check up on them very often. They are too lazy to bribe kids to pose in front of a sign or to send a newsletter. They achieve expert level at computer games and movie trivia.

5% – Started with good intentions but lost their faith, or at least their zeal. They are not interested in going to church themselves or encouraging others in their faith. They stay overseas because the paychecks keep coming and they don't see an alternative. They love to philosophize and complain. This group can sap the life out of you like a dementor in *Harry Potter*.

80% – Decent, hard-working Christians–the kind who would volunteer to teach the 3rd and 4th grade Sunday School class in your church year after year. This is the group that we aspired to belong to.

After a few months of not paying much attention to the fakes, Kim's faith returned. I had more problems with the heroes. They had great language ability, insights, and ministries, and I knew I didn't measure up. I looked for ways to criticize them behind their backs and pull them down to my level of mediocrity.

Despite our intentions to identify with locals, we dissipated far too much energy on expats. I had significant conflicts with four men. Three times I made a phone call, said, "Let's have lunch and talk," and resolved the conflicts. The fourth time I thought my chance of success was so close to zero that I didn't make the call. It was a slow and painful process learning to ignore the bad apples, respect the heroes, appreciate our friends, mind our own business, shut up, and do our work.

Last year we went to Washington state to visit our linguist friends, who have also moved back to the US. We took along some good coffee, but they already had plenty.

16 MEAT IS BACK ON THE MENU

"... possibly the deepest human need is the need to be appreciated " Gary Chapman, The Five Love Languages

The premise of Gary Chapman's excellent book, *The Five Love Languages*, is that people express and understand love in different ways. For example, a father may communicate love to his adult daughter by repairing her car; she may be yearning for him to express his love in words. When they understand the concept of love languages, she can appreciate his unspoken love and he can try to overcome his inhibitions to verbalize it.

In the minority cultures of rural China, one of the significant ways you express love and appreciation for people is by killing an animal and feeding it to them. We had been shown love with fresh chicken, goat, mutton, pork, and beef. So one summer we raised a pig, and sent out dinner invitations to 30 friends.

Living most of my life in rural Idaho, I had butchered scores of farm and big game animals, including 20 pigs. But I had never needed to kill an active 240-pound animal with a knife before. It happened without a plan-of-the-day meeting or a pre-job safety briefing. Little Bird, her teenage husband, Ahma, and I were loitering around the pigpen, talking about firewood. Without warning Ahma grabbed the boar by the hind leg and said, "Let's get started!" Pigs are smart animals and he knew what was going down. He thrashed and knocked her sprawling, sending her enormous black hat into the mud. The other three of us dived on and I yelled for Niels to bring the butcher knife. I inserted it above the sternum and pushed it down through the bristly thick muddy skin into the heart. The bright red blood spurted into a blue plastic dishpan. The pig squealed as four of us pinned his warm and dying body. Dropping a mule deer from 300 yards with one shot can make you feel like a skilled sniper. Kneeling on a squealing, intelligent animal as you make sure the blade hits his heart can make you feel like a killer. I hated everything about it.

As I cut up the meat I said politely, "I have always enjoyed everything we have eaten in the villages, but there are some parts of a pig I don't know how to prepare. Would you like to have them?"

"Like what?" they asked.

Well, the skin. "What?! That's one of the best parts!"

And the head. "What?! That's what you should serve to the most honored guest!"

And the blood. "What?! Then how do you make sausage?"

Thanks, that reminds me. Not the intestines either. "What?! Do all Americans waste the best parts of a pig?"

Five or six people had a discerning look at the pig's gall bladder and informed me happily that it was large and full, which indicated our business would make a lot of money in the next year[22].

We had guests from four countries and four different Chinese minority groups. Some honored guests were the scholarship students funded by Mountain Friends, including some girls who otherwise probably wouldn't have learned how to read. We played basketball and ping pong, ate local style pork soup, rice, peanuts, oranges, and American-style BBQ ribs. Conversation topics ranged from firewood prices (skyrocketing!), to the cost of sending kids to junior high (going down!), to vegetarians (really strange!), to points of doctrine in our various religions.

---

[22] Our business, Skirts and Daggers, which exported minority crafts to the US and sold them there, didn't make money that year or any other year. Never trust a gall bladder with sales projections.

Another time we had a party for 25 Nosu high school students and 10 other guests. Fortunately lacking a pig to kill, we prepared 90 chicken drumsticks and 12 pounds of pork from the market. After eating our fill, I told the students I had two hopes for their future.

One hope was they would value their cultural history, traditions, and elders. The Nosu are often described by the other ethnic groups as stupid, dirty thieves and are routinely despised or ignored. I had invited Teacher Lu, the Nosu Renaissance Man, to come in from his village and tell traditional stories. He told legends about Zhygge Alur, who shot six of the seven suns out of the sky and made the world cool enough for crops to grow. He told about the Creator sending four angels to assist in creation, one each for the North, South, East, and West parts of the world. I asked the students if they had heard these stories already and they said, "Of course, but never told as well as this!"

I told the students my second hope for them was they would learn to be open-minded—to listen to and understand stories from other times and places. An American friend told the story of the Lost Son, how he defied his Father, squandered his youth and wealth, and was so hungry he wanted to eat pig food. The students were listening intently to the story and there was laughter at the part about the pig food. When the Father showed amazing grace for his rebellious son and joyfully accepted him back, there was a sigh of relief. I asked if they had heard that story already, and they all said, "No, never, but it is very interesting!"

Some students volunteered to tell their own stories. One told of his grandparents falling in love despite being in a caste system that would not allow their marriage. They fled their homes in Sichuan province and married in Yunnan. The students spontaneously sang song after plaintive song in the Nosu language, about love and hope. In the evening, they sang a song to thank us and returned to school for a mandatory Saturday study hall.

Minority high school students had a hard life. They lived in dorm rooms with 20 roommates, with no furniture except rows of bunk beds. Someone was always sick and coughing and it was hard for anyone to get enough sleep. They had class or study hall seven days a week. They barely had free time or spending money. They were learning their subjects in a difficult second language (Chinese) and studying a baffling third language (English). The other kids made fun of them for their funny accents and lack of money. We couldn't do much for most of them. But that Saturday, they could eat as much meat as they wanted, know they were respected, and that we appreciated their stories. Sometimes listening communicates as much love as bacon.

Silly Americans; the skin is delicious!

17 TORCH FESTIVAL

"Other people, however, possess equally strange customs, which provide analogies to the gospel." Don Richardson, Eternity in Their Hearts

Ironically, once Kim and I had an argument about *Peace Child.*

It is a classic missions book about Don Richardson's outreach to the Sawi people in Papua New Guinea (PNG) in 1962. It is one of the best and best-selling missions books of all time, and it brought the idea of the redemptive analogy[23] into the mainstream. It is also an encouraging and well-written story, and I suspect we were the first married couple in history to argue about it.

I started it, by telling Kim, "I studied the timeline in the book, and when Don Richardson was explaining how the Sawi concept of a Peace Child provided an analogy to Christ's sacrifice, he had only been studying the language for about five months. How can you explain a metaphorical religious concept with grunts and hand motions? And in the epilogue, where he describes his happy wife and happy kids playing happily with happy Sawi people, he lets on his family has been in PNG all the

---

[23] For example, the New Testament calls Jesus a "sacrificial lamb," using the language of the Jewish Passover.

time. I bet they spent most of those years in an air conditioned missions compound in Australia."

Kim said, "Maybe his language learning aptitude was better than ours, and certainly he worked harder at it. And you have no idea how long his family was in PNG. Give them the benefit of the doubt unless you actually know. It is OK to let people be heroes without trying to tear them down."

To gain more ammo for my irrational attack on Don Richardson, I read another of his books, *Eternity in Their Hearts*.

The big idea of this book is many cultures throughout history, from the Jews to the Greeks to the Incas, have cultural traditions which prepare them to understand the good news of Christ's death paying the penalty for their sins.

As do the Nosu.

On the 24th day of the 6th month of the lunar calendar, using a date which was probably derived from the 10-month Yi solar calendar[24], the Nosu celebrate the torch festival.

Each family selects a lamb and the head of the household lifts it over the head of each person in the family. The sins[25] of each person are transferred to the lamb and it is killed.

A torch is lit in front of each home. A big bonfire is lit in the village square and there is singing and dancing. We've been told all kinds of versions of the origin and meaning of the torch festival.

"The torches light the way so the good spirits can find the village and come to bless us."

"The torches are used to drive away unclean spirits."

"The ceremony with the lamb is the most important thing a Nosu person can take part in each year."

"Once a long time ago there was a plague of insects, and

---

[24] If you are an engineer like me, you probably don't need any more conversation killers in your bag of tricks. But if you do, study up on obscure calendars.

[25] It is notoriously difficult to agree on a cross cultural definition of sin, and to be consistent in translation. Some cultures emphasize guilt, and sin has more to do with violating an objective moral law. Other cultures emphasize shame, and sin has more to do with violating right relationships.

someone came up with the idea of using fire to drive them away; unbelievably, it worked, and the village didn't starve. So each year we light the torches to commemorate that event and to drive away any insects."

We celebrated the torch festival with our friends in the villages several times. Once we had a team from Idaho with us, and we did line dancing and singing into the night. We did Nosu dances and we sang "Amazing Grace," and the mountains echoed with new friendships.

A Nosu friend said, "We have often had outsiders come into our village during the torch festival and try to take photos of us, but we have never had outsiders come into our village and sing and dance with us like old friends."

An American friend said, "I feel like I just became part of a National Geographic special."

I wanted to say, "Hey! Sacrificial lambs, sin, forgiveness! This is a redemptive analogy!" But my language was still not good enough to say "redemptive analogy," and no one understood my grunts and hand gestures. I had no more shade to throw at Don Richardson, and the marital argument ended as most should— with the husband's apology.

18 SENDING THE SOULS TO HEAVEN

"Nothing is more often misdiagnosed than our homesickness for Heaven. We think that what we want is sex, drugs, alcohol, a new job, a raise, a doctorate, a spouse, a large screen TV, a new car, a cabin in the woods, a condo in Hawaii. What we really want is the person we were made for, Jesus, and the place we were made for, Heaven. Nothing less can satisfy us." Randy Alcorn, Heaven

A Nosu child's greatest responsibility is to send their parent's soul to heaven. The four day ceremony was in a village three hours away. A grandmother and grandfather we knew had both died and been cremated there in the past couple of years. I went to represent Ahma, who wouldn't go to any ceremonies where her ex-husband was present. I ended up sharing a room with him. He was an alcoholic, and after Ahma divorced him, he had moved in with his shrill mistress. Every night of the funeral, he and another drunkard would stagger in about 2 AM and pass out in the bed next to me.

The ceremony was conducted by the local bimo. Bimos have collections of cloth scrolls written in the pictographic Nosu script. I had a friend in the village, a schoolteacher about my age, who spoke good Chinese. He explained to me what was done and what it symbolized.

We met first in a log cabin, dirt floor, with about 50 people attending. The bimo began by reciting genealogies and lists of surviving family. Young men built a bonfire of green branches and pine needles in the doorway to deliberately fill the cabin with smoke. Two junior high boys brought in a sheep and struggled to hold him. All of the close family members knelt in the doorway as the bimo lifted the sheep and passed it over their heads, one by one. Then the boys held the sheep on the floor and the bimo killed it with a knife. My friend said it was a kind of purification ritual. Other young men quickly butchered the sheep. They laid the liver directly in the coals and placed the meat and innards in a huge wok in the center of the cabin. About 11 PM dinner was served.

The next day all of the ceremonies took place outdoors. At first light firecrackers popped to summon us outside. A male representative of each child's and grandchild's family came leading a sheep. One grandchild was a widow, so she had to bring a six-year-old son so there would be a male representative. There were seven families and sheep in all. One by one the family members led the sheep in front of the bimo while he chanted words from the scrolls. Two men ceremoniously knocked the sheep on the head with a chunk of firewood, killed them with a knife, and carefully arranged the bodies in a straight line. The line went from the bimo to some household items like bowls, liquor, and rice. The bimo took a live chicken and passed it through the legs of the dead sheep, and sprinkled some rice, chanting loudly all the while. My friend said this ceremony was to ensure the departed would have good food to eat in heaven.

On the third day the ceremony continued outdoors. The bimo poked 180 fresh cut tree branches in the ground, upright in intersecting lines. He tethered a live goat at the end of the longest line. The bimo took some hot stones out of the bonfires and arranged them within the branches. Two men held the goat upside down and used it to knock down every one of the branches. Then a small boy took the tether and he and the goat skipped away happily. Of course, the bimo was chanting and reciting loudly all the time. My friend said this procedure helps the departed spirits choose the right path to heaven. A loose translation of the chanting: "Choose the right path, don't go down the wrong path; choose the white path, don't go down the dark path!"

Then a representative from each extended family, including me, did a ceremony to wish the departed the best in the afterlife. We all filed past the bimo and received a sip of whiskey, a boiled egg, some grains of rice, and a piece of candy—which we consumed on the spot. The bimo took all of the leftover rice and candy and flung it over his shoulder, whereupon everyone boisterously scrambled to pick it up. It was something like throwing the garter at an American wedding, except all ages and both genders took part.

One of the old men cut a short bamboo tube, split it lengthwise, and used a knife to dig out a hole the size of a marble. The bimo fashioned a tiny grass figure representing the departed and put it in the tube. The old man slowly laced the tube back together. The bimo choose two men to carry the bamboo into the mountains and hide it in a cave.

When the men came back after depositing the bamboo tube, the bimo recited some more and said the souls were safely in heaven. There was a general atmosphere of celebration. He said grandfather and grandmother wanted to give a blessing for our health. Their wish was for everyone to smoke cigarettes together. So all of us, from about age six on up, filed past and received one cigarette. We took them back to the bonfires and lit them. I was with a group of young people, including two pretty girls about eight years old. They lit their cigarettes solemnly in the coals, but after a puff they started coughing and giggling. Since we all know laughter is good for you, they probably received the health blessing after all.

A funeral procession.

19 DEVELOPMENT

"Asia is not going to be civilized by the methods of the West. There is too much Asia and she is too old." Rudyard Kipling

We learned to do development work from trial and error and a wise Japanese man, who was my supervisor with Food for the Hungry. Their development model required community involvement in exchange for financial investment. We never gave away money or material without the recipients contributing something, such as labor.

We taught English classes but the students had to pay, at least a little. We installed a clean water system at a village school, but the parents provided the labor to cap the spring and run the pipe down the mountainside. We gave scholarships to help girls stay in school, but never for the full tuition—the parents always had to provide something.

There were always unintended consequences. In a village school several hours away, an Australian linguist noticed the 20 or so Nosu kids at the boarding school, some as young as six, were sleeping on dirt floors and cooking on a wood fire, sometimes burning themselves. So he compassionately raised money for bunk beds and a cook stove. The next semester all of the Nosu kids dropped out of school and faded back into the mountains. He didn't know why and asked me to go with him to find out.

We found the kids in a village about five miles away, not attending school at all, and one of the parents explained. "When the school got the great stuff you bought for the dormitory, they had to have someone there to make sure it didn't get stolen. So they hired a girl to cook and watch the dorms. Her salary had to come from somewhere, so the school started charging each student about $5 per semester. We couldn't afford it, so we pulled the kids out of school." The linguist started a scholarship program.

There was another Nosu village where three guys made traditional lacquerware crafts. We took groups to their shop and the groups always bought enough to fill their backpacks. So I started a company called Skirts and Daggers, bought lacquerware and some other crafts, exported them to the US, and sold[26] them from skirtsanddaggers.com. We were so good for the lacquerware business the artisans killed a sheep and invited us out for a meal.

Not long after that an Australian post doc and a person from the Chinese small business administration got wind of the shop. They held the craftsmen up as examples of what happens when minorities value their traditions and gave them a grant worth about $1500. The three guys got drunk, got in an argument about how to split up the money, and to my knowledge, never made another bowl.

Another non-profit came through doing eye exams and handing out free eyeglasses to whoever needed them. The young people in the village were miffed the old people were getting more free stuff than they were, so they intentionally failed their eye exams, got the free glasses, and wore them, even though it made their vision worse.

I laid the groundwork for a Village School Assistance Program. With the planning typical of an engineer, I developed a schedule, a budget, and a pronounceable acronym. (How's the funding for VeeSAP this year?)The school teacher was often the only literate person in the village, was a representative of the government, and had considerable influence for a single twenty-

---

[26] "Advertised" would be more accurate. Sales were sluggish.

something. My program was to provide materials and resources to the teachers, visit them periodically, and gain legitimate access to several villages. Right as I was about to launch, the local Education Department closed all of the one-room village schools and moved the students and teachers to centralized boarding schools. The ramshackle schools, windows broken, doors flapping in the wind, no longer had teachers in need of assistance.

It is fatalistic nonsense to say because development projects sometimes fail, or have unintended consequences, they are not worth doing. But the failures should motivate us to think through the process and refine our methods.

Some projects we helped with did have long-lasting benefits:

• Scholarships for girls to stay in school through junior high and high school. Studies and common sense indicate literate girls make better mothers. It is good to read stories to your small children and directions on bottles of medicine. Literate girls are also less likely to be exploited because they can get jobs if necessary. Better mothers make better communities.

• Projects that provided clean drinking water. Studies and common sense show drinking clean water has immediate and dramatic health benefits.

• Projects that provided centralized village latrines. In 2004 even some larger Nosu villages we visited, with a couple hundred people, did not have any household toilets or village latrines. People used ditches and the hillside and often had gastrointestinal problems as a result.

• Projects that provided health screenings and immunizations.

• Projects that helped village medical clinics gain access to commonly used medicines, like those on the World Health Organization's List of Essential Medicines.

Not all unintended consequences were negative. When we traveled to visit schools we often took Anna and Niels with us, and locals commented on the benefits of our parenting methods and asked us to explain. We weren't trying to organize Dare to Discipline parenting seminars, but sometimes they just happened.

People are all the same. An illiterate street sweeper may have a higher IQ than you or me. But cultures are different. All cultures have things that can and should change, and development workers are change agents. We should respect the locals, hold them in equal value, and have the courage to work together to change what is needed.

20 TEAMS

"Talent wins games, but teamwork and intelligence wins championships." Michael Jordan

One of our roles was to host teams from the US and organize two-week English camps. Kim and I wrote a curriculum and developed a format in which a team leader would spend several hours each day with a small group of students. The students were typically 14-21 years old, had studied English in school, but never had a conversation with a native speaker.

We taught them to sing "Amazing Grace" and "Eight Days a Week." We talked about food and goals for the future. The small group leaders and their students would usually find common ground and there would be copious tears and promises to write letters when they said good-bye.

The content of the camps was honestly pretty good and we used it 11 times with teams from Idaho, Kentucky, and Arizona. We passed it on and a couple of organizations continue to use it to this day.

Most of the teams were from churches and were part of their short-term missions programs. We were humbled by having 12 or so talented, hard-working, well-prepared people use most or all of their yearly vacation to help us teach English.

One year we arranged for the visiting teachers to stay in one of the newer hotels, at $35 per night per room. A local person, if they couldn't stay with extended family, would find accommodations for $2 per night, so the new hotel was mostly used by wealthier tourists and Chinese businessmen. Like many hotels in Asia, management had a working relationship with some prostitutes, who would go through the halls, knocking softly on the doors at bedtime to find clients.

One of the men from our home church, an elder who had his 10-year-old son along, had a light bulb burn out in his room. He dialed the front desk and let them know. "We'll send someone to fix it."

A few minutes later there was a knock on his door. As he explained it the next morning, he was puzzled the hotel maintenance person was wearing makeup and a very short skirt. The hooker saw his earnest demeanor and young son and knew there had been a mistake. She came into his room, worked on the light bulb, smiled, and left. The next morning at our team meeting we serenaded him with another Beatles song, "Money Can't Buy You Love."

Another time I mentioned in a newsletter, as a matter of cultural and biological interest, that we had a rat living in the outdoor squatty potty at our home. Once as I went #1, he popped up out of the drain, damp headed, gave me an indignant look, and scuttled out the door. I did not realize hearing this story would cause at least one visiting team member to become apprehensive about using all Eastern toilets, stop drinking water to the point of dehydration, and develop a painful stomachache.

Another team heard, accurately, that many public restrooms in China do not have toilet paper and that you should take your own with you. Using a part-to-whole fallacy, they generalized this to "there is an inadequate amount of toilet paper in China" and solved the problem by bringing an extra checked bag, a big one on rollers, containing nothing but Charmin.

Usually in the English camps our students were local kids, with sunburned faces and weather-beaten clothes. One year the Chinese Justin Bieber attended. He wasn't actually a pop star, but he was a city boy from Kunming who looked like one. The girls swooned. He had milk white skin and long hair like you see on a shampoo commercial[27]. One day after lunch we returned to find patrol cars outside and several police in our classroom. Jealousy over which girl had the inside track with the heartthrob had turned into a face slapping gang fight, and one of the girls had called the police on her cell phone.

In the past two decades the number of long-term missionaries from Western countries has declined slightly, but the number of short-term teams has exploded. Some long termers deride short termers behind their backs, but are nice to them in person, because they depend on their donations for funding. Some long-termers don't appreciate anyone knowing what they are doing overseas, or not doing. Some long-termers partner with teams in ways that benefit both, as well as the locals.

Teams are a reality. They can provide specialized skills, energy, and accountability[28]. They were a terrific encouragement to us and working with them was one of the high points of each year. We also had five different young women stay with us from 2-5 months each. They weren't nannies; they were friends who became like family members, and they were also a tremendous blessing to us. If you are living overseas, and have the chance to host an intelligent young person, full of curiosity and *joie de vivre*, say "yes" with your next breath.

In our original pro-con list for whether we were willing to go to China, one of our biggest cons had been "give up our friendships in Idaho." But we had underestimated the quality of our friends. They supported us financially, wrote to us, and joined teams to come see our lives and help us. Instead of eroding our friendships, our being overseas added another dimension to them, and they are stronger today than ever.

During trips to the US, there were always opportunities to give updates and presentations. I spoke at churches, schools, and because we did so much hiking, the Idaho Falls Alpine Club. One year I spoke to about 5,000 different people. After speaking about China and the Nosu I would say "Does anyone

---

[27] He was about 17 years old, 5'1" and 80 lbs., but when has that ever mattered to teenage girls?

[28] And boxes of homeschool books and baking chocolate.

have a question?" Occasionally an overachiever would ask one on topic, but mostly the questions were like this:

In Riggins, Idaho, from a grizzled logger, "Didja know we have wolves in the mountains now?"

In Plummer, Idaho, from a Native American I used to play basketball with, "You still got your hops?"

From a high school student, "How long have you lived in like, Japan?"

And, inevitably, "So, did you eat a lot of Chinese food, ha ha ha?"

Once I was preparing for a presentation and saw a sweet 60 year-old lady who received our newsletters, but had not seen me in person for very long time. She ran forward, prepared to give me a hug, looked me up and down, and then burst into tears. "What *happened* to you?" she said, "Did living in China give you a tropical disease?" I tried to reassure her that I don't eat a lot of sugar, exercise regularly, have been thin since high school, and actually, I always look this way.

I've been on both sides of the church/missionary relationship. I led the missions team at church for six years, where we supported about 10 families. My family was supported by four different churches for the seven years we were overseas.

Theologically, churches are Christ's bride that He loved and died for. The universal church will exist for all eternity. Missions agencies are temporary organizations with special skills, like language and culture expertise. I saw this akin to a general contractor/subcontractor relationship. Financially, churches and their members mostly control how and where the money flows.

Some people see missionaries as heroes, as the best Christians, and hold them up as examples to emulate. Some see them as non-stop fundraisers and reflexively put a guarding hand on their wallets when a missionary shows up at Bible study. Rarely are missionaries treated as fundamentally normal humans.

I believe short-term teams contribute to the unrealistic view, because in two weeks overseas, you can live on an adrenaline rush of exotic experiences and idealism. After two months the adrenaline high is fading, and after two years the novelty is way long gone. Which is why, when you go to visit, you should give your host an extra bag of good coffee.

Tibetan girls at an English camp.

21 BELIEVERS IN THE MIDDLE KINGDOM

"In an age of hedonism and corruption, selfless activism has helped the [Chinese] churches' reputation; not least, it has persuaded the regime that Christians are not out to overthrow it." Rob Gifford, in The Economist

From 1980 to 2010 the number of Chinese Christians increased from about 1 million to about 100 million. The magnitude and velocity of this increase is unheard of in religion or in physics. If you drew a vector it would look like an arrow pointing toward heaven.

Some believe that China's economic explosion during those same decades was fueled by Christian work ethic and willingness to trust business partners outside of family bonds. Chinese believers are known for showing up, working, and not stealing, which are minimum essentials for business everywhere.

This rapid growth in the Christian church has not been evenly distributed throughout the country. Especially in the rural minority areas, many people in 2004 had never met a Christian or heard of Jesus.

The Nosu were even less fortunate. In the 1990's a cult called the Mentuhui (Discipleship Society) swept through and confusion followed in its wake. Disciples were told if they had one egg and enough faith, there would be two eggs in the morning. If they jumped off a cliff and had enough faith, they could fly. If a member died and their family had enough faith, he or she would be brought back to life. Apparently many disciples lacked faith, because following the religion often resulted in hunger, broken bones, and rotting corpses. The government placed the Mentuhui on the list of illegal religions, as the unburied bodies were a public health hazard.

The Mentuhui adapted by calling themselves *Jidutu* (Christians). Christianity *is* legal in China, although unregistered churches are not. When we arrived and were asked our religion and said Jidutu, the assumption by some was that we were nutjobs in the cult where people thought they could fly.

For most people in traditional cultures around the world, there is no need to go through a logical argument to convince them that there is more to life than time, chemistry, and chance. They have heard the grotesque voices, seen the vacant eyes, and experienced the superhuman hyperactivity of someone afflicted by an evil spirit, and been outdoors under the stars enough nights to be convinced of the reality of a Creator. Their question is not, "Is there a God?" but, "Is Jesus, whom you seem to keep bringing up, more powerful than the spirits we are familiar with?"

Many conversations with locals had me saying something like, "No, I'm not afraid of the spirits in that bend of the river, or in that grove of trees. Jesus is more powerful than whatever is in there."

When requested, we passed around some Christian material such as recordings of parts of the Nosu New Testament. It became clear to those who listened that this was different than the Mentuhui cult, but that dealing with Jesus was still not easy and required a decision. Mock him or worship him? Ignore him or memorize every word he said?

Our Nosu friends do not make decisions the same way Americans do. We are individuals in individual families; they are part of a clan. When they talked about becoming Christians, they talked about it as a group decision. One weekend, as we were told much later, a group of about 80 listened to the New Testament for several hours, then had a discussion about whether to become followers of Jesus. Among many others,

Little Bird and Ahma spoke in favor; Little Bird's brother spoke against.

The consensus was that the current generation should stay with the old ways, but the next generation could be Christian. So when Little Bird gave birth to a daughter, she asked us to give her a Christian name and help raise her as a believer, which we were overjoyed to do. We chose Lydia—the name of a woman mentioned in the Bible who had a church that met in her home.

Were we missionaries? It is not legal to be a missionary in China so that was never our official role. We always had other legitimate roles we worked hard at, like development and teaching ESL.

We didn't do what many would associate with missions work. We didn't start a church or teach at a seminary. I have never started a church or taught at a seminary in the US, and it would be unrealistic to think that could happen in a few years considering my lack of training, lack of ability, lack of excellent Chinese, let alone lack of excellent Nosu.

We were active believers, as many of you are. We frequently spoke with Nosu people about coming to faith and prayed for that to happen. Several of our Nosu friends did make professions of faith and continue to believe.

Most people are missionaries for something, whether they recognize it or not—be it fitness, hedonism, conservative values, liberal values, protecting the environment, good beer, philosophic naturalism, golf, or Jesus.

Christianity is one of many worldviews competing in the free marketplace of ideas. Not all ideas are equally valid, and objective reality underlies them all. If you smoke cigarettes you are more likely to get lung cancer than if you don't, regardless of whether you believe it or not. I believe health is better than sickness, wealth is better than poverty, education is better than ignorance, love is better than hate, and following Jesus is better than living in fear of demons and ghosts.

Although I am careful—maybe too careful—to not talk about Jesus with people who aren't interested, I don't apologize for desiring every person on earth to hear of Him, His claims, and deal with Him themselves.

Almost everyone I know thinks the world is getting progressively worse. I think in my lifetime, 1963-2017, it has gotten better, and fast. When I have this argument, I usually point to three things[29].

1) Global life expectancy has increased from about 50 years to about 70 years.

2) Worldwide literacy has grown from less than 60% to greater than 80%.

3) This chart:

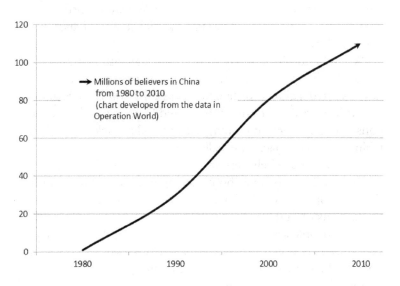

An arrow pointing towards heaven.

---

[29] My friends usually start by pointing to public morality—for example by comparing *The Andy Griffith Show* to *Two and a Half Men*. Point taken, but is American prime time TV really a good metric for whether the whole world is a better place?

22 LOSING LYDIA AND HOPE

"Little girls are cute and small only to adults. To one another they are not cute. They are life-sized." Margaret Atwood

This chapter was originally sent as a newsletter in November 2008.

We have written before about a Nosu girl we call Little Bird. We met her two weeks after our arrival in China four years ago. She has been our cook, language teacher, landlord and friend. Three months before we met her, when she was 19, she had been forced to marry a 14-year-old boy. Almost all Nosu marriages are arranged and the girl has little say.

She protested vehemently and has tried twice to get a divorce. Both attempts were denied and when her husband was 17 they moved in together. The next year a beautiful baby girl was born. Kim and I were honored to be her godparents and to give her her Christian name: Lydia. Lydia has become a part of our family. She plays in our kitchen every afternoon. She prefers Kim to anyone in the world except her mother. Even when her grandfather comes to visit, she runs to Kim to hold her. All the local people are amazed a little Nosu girl can have such a close relationship with her foreign godmother.

I also love to play with Lydia. We build block towers and she crashes them down and laughs. She loves to play dress up and admire herself in the mirror. We are teaching her English, so I made up a song: "I'm as pretty as my earring, I'm as pretty as my curl, I'm as pretty as my necklace, I'm a pretty little girl." (She says ee-wing for earring.)

Anna said last week, "I've always wanted a little sister, and I think Lydia works great!"

We have lived on the same property with Little Bird and her husband for two years and we knew that their relationship has never been good. They have often fought verbally and sometimes physically. He is lazy and passive; she is demanding and has a fierce temper.

Last week his family initiated divorce proceedings. A Nosu divorce involves both sides bringing together their extended families. The two families assemble relatively close but are not allowed to see each other, to prevent open violence. A group of impartial go-betweens travels back and forth with offers and counteroffers as the two sides negotiate.

Part of the negotiation is financial. A husband who divorces his wife normally is required to pay several thousand dollars. The other part of the negotiation is custody of the children. Typically children go to the father's side. But this was an unusual case. Little Bird has more energy and ambition than her husband, and so has better prospects for making money and supporting a family. Also, Lydia's relationship with our family is unique. No Nosu child has ever grown up with a foreign family and had the opportunity to learn English from the cradle. And her baby sister is less than a month old. It shouldn't be possible to take a tiny nursing baby away from her mother. There is no such thing as joint custody. The other side of the family is not allowed even to visit the child until they enter school. The stakes in a custody case are all or nothing.

About 10 days ago extended family started arriving. We hosted 10 people and Little Bird hosted another 20. A requirement for hosting out of town guests is to kill an animal for them on the day of their arrival. The go-betweens also require a freshly butchered animal. So Little Bird traded a big hog for a calf and two sheep. We all ate the calf together last Saturday night. The atmosphere was almost festive. After three days the negotiations moved out to a village, and the number of extended family swelled to 200. More animals were killed. We did not go to the village but received daily updates from Little Bird's family.

"The go-betweens said their family needs to give our family $30,000 dollars!"

"They don't want either of the girls; we get both of them!"

Rumors were flying. Our family skipped a meal so that we could fast and pray for a peaceful, just outcome.

Yesterday many of the extended family returned home. The women were crying, the men slumped and silent. Little Bird's older sister ran to me and grabbed my hands, tears pouring.

"We lost everything! They took both of the girls!"

Little Bird walked past in shock, supported by her mother. We were in disbelief and questions poured out.

"Can't you go to the government authorities?"

"No, there was never a legal civil marriage, only a traditional tribal ceremony."

"What if we moved and you sold this house we rented from you? We are certainly willing to do that. Would that generate enough money to get Lydia back?"

"No, mostly it is not about the house or the money; it is about 'face.' If my husband's family gives up the children they lose face."

"Couldn't you go to the Chinese police?"

"No, the police would consider it a minority issue, and they wouldn't get involved."

"You know our family has connections. Would that help?"

"No, his family said if we used any of your connections to get Lydia, or if we took her back by force, they would wait and burn our house down some night with Lydia inside. That isn't just a threat; they would do it."

"We had a pretty good relationship with your husband. Couldn't we go to the village ourselves and see Lydia and talk with him?"

"No, they would think that you are trying to find a way to get her back. They would definitely harm one of my family or one of our children. Please don't go out and try to see her or take things into your own hands."

"Isn't there anything we can do to help you get the girls back?"

"There is nothing you can do."

And there is nothing we can do.

So Lydia and her baby sister, Hope, are gone. Little Bird went to the hospital last night because of the physical pain from suddenly stopping nursing, and because her mother thought the emotional pain could give her a heart attack.

So here we are in 2008, in the modern world. We are rich, powerful Americans, used to making things happen, used to getting our way. We are using a DSL connection in our home to send a report of a tribal feud that has ripped our hearts out. And there is nothing we can do to get the little girls back.

Little Bird, Kim, Hope and Lydia on the day before the little girls were taken.

23 HEARTBREAK

"Everyone has a plan till they get punched in the mouth." Mike Tyson

Our Chinese was good enough to understand almost everything people said to us. I'd learned enough characters to read most of the way through the New Testament. We were healthy, homeschool was thriving, I had an occasional Bible study going with some Nosu friends. Anna and Niels each had a best friend in China and lots more good friends. We enjoyed the outdoors and village trips to see people like Teacher Lu. Our scholarship program was humming and we enjoyed the favor of many local people. I had made peace with the expats in town and took turns speaking at the foreigners' fellowship about once a month.

The tagline for this book mentions Heartbreak and Hope on China's Tibetan Frontier. You may have guessed the events of the last chapter, where a stupid clan feud resulted in Lydia and Hope being taken from their mother and from us, are part of the heartbreak[30].

After the little girls were taken, Kim and I began to develop a rift. She kept coming up with ideas for how to resolve the issue

---

[30] The part about China's Tibetan frontier? That is just there to attract attention and increase sales. Remember 50% of the profits go to a good cause.

and get them back, and I kept coming up with objections for why her ideas wouldn't work. I felt inadequate and incompetent. When a husband feels incompetent and gets tired of listening to his wife's ideas, trouble is brewing. When he tells her please don't bring up the topic again, the trouble has fully brewed and is ready to drink.

There was not open conflict in our home. We continued to work together well to homeschool Anna and Niels. We continued to go for walks together and enjoy good meals and friendships, and we continued to enjoy sharing a bedroom.[31] We didn't raise our voices with each other.

But different issues kept falling into the rift and preventing it from closing. The primary one was learning Chinese. Kim had wanted to spend our first two or three years in dedicated language study at a university. I believed we could use local tutors and learn Chinese at the same time we did development projects, taught English, and made friends. Kim wanted us to consider having Anna and Niels go to Chinese public school, which would have given her time away from homeschooling to do her own language study. I agreed that everyone's language ability would have improved, but I said, "Language is not the only consideration. You do homeschool better than anyone else does anything, and I don't think we should give that up for the sake of language study." So not only would I not agree to the public school idea, I wouldn't consider it or discuss it.

Another point of contention was how to teach someone who is a new Christian the essentials of the theology and practice of the faith. The insider word for this is discipleship. I believed that it was possible to do discipleship the same way as evangelism— by being friends, spending time together, and answering questions as they came up naturally. Kim believed that discipleship should be intentional and done in a systematic way.

---

[31] The bedrooms weren't heated and the temperature indoors sometimes dropped below freezing. We used old down sleeping bags covered with wool blankets to stay warm. The effect this has on intimacy is like when you sit in the hot springs at Loon Creek, then jump in the icy water of the stream. There are dramatic temperature variations, but the overall effect is one that you look forward to repeating.

She wanted to do regular teaching of our friends who had made professions of faith, but she didn't feel her language ability was adequate. Since my homeschool teaching load was lighter, I had had more time for language study, so Kim thought I should teach our friends. I got my back up and refused, more out of conviction that Kim shouldn't tell me what to do than conviction about ministry methodology.

There was also an undercurrent of tension in our home due to the continuing clan feud. There were rumors that what the other side really wanted was the property, not the two girls, and they were planning to burn down the houses out of spite, with us inside. Arson was a common occurrence in Nosu clan feuds. I was in one village where several houses had been burned to the ground. We took the threat seriously, staged rope ladders at the bedroom windows, and had family fire drills, without telling Anna and Niels about the specific threats.

Kim and I didn't have a single argument while we were dating, and no real ones our first five years of marriage. We never had a disagreement about money. We never worried that the other was interested in another person, physically or mentally. We believed that the fact we had a great marriage meant we were great at communication and conflict resolution. In fact, we had rarely been tested, and we were terrible at it.

The fundamentals of marriage are for the husband to love his wife, the wife to respect her husband, and for them to be willing to sincerely apologize and forgive each other when they mess up. All of these fundamentals were eroding. I felt Kim's respect drying up as I didn't listen to her ideas about the lost little girls, language study, and ministry. When she lamented that after four years her language wasn't where she thought it would be, I didn't love her. I said, in a superior tone, "You know, *your* problem is that your expectations were unrealistic. If you look at the Foreign Service scale, and the number of hours you have had for language learning, you are actually above average. I wish you would be grateful for what you do have and not regret what you don't." We continued to think poorly of each other, and not forgive.

The tagline about Heartbreak? That was also happening to

us.

Leaving on our honeymoon, 1988.

24 ON THE REBOUND

"The definition of second marriage is the triumph of hope over experience." George Will

Most Nosu people have engagements that last a decade. Zeyi has been engaged to his cousin since first grade. They are expected to marry after both of them finish college. But Little Bird had a much shorter second engagement.

<u>Wednesday</u>: Ahma told us, "There might be a few people coming over from Sichuan to talk about arranging a marriage with Little Bird."

<u>Thursday</u>: Two uncles arrived and began negotiations.

<u>Friday morning</u>: They agreed to a deal, and Older Brother came into town and killed one of the pigs. Ahma said, "We're going to have an engagement party here tonight."

<u>Friday evening</u>: Sixty people were at our house. We were not convinced the marriage was a good plan and still hadn't met the young man. But no matter. Pork was roasting, beer was flowing, music was pumping. Niels got a ping-pong tournament going. Some of the men from the villages, unused to outhouses, were going pee in random places, including our courtyard. We carried tables into our sunroom for a meal and spread out pads upstairs for overflow sleeping space. Little Bird's sister was very excited about the match. She boiled 40 eggs in our kitchen and told Kim, "Eat an egg; it shows that you agree with the marriage!"

Kim hadn't agreed to the marriage and wouldn't eat the egg. Older Sister chased Kim around the kitchen, trying to get her to eat it. Neither of these intelligent, opinionated women were laughing. Kim eventually diplomatically took an egg but only put it in her pocket.

Saturday morning: We met the prospective groom. I have a theory you can learn more about someone's character in one hour of pick-up basketball than in a year of conversations. I arranged a few games, making sure he would win some and lose some. We split some wood together. Kim and I watched him and Little Bird interacting.

Saturday afternoon: Ahma told us happily, "The old people have done a divination on the lucky dates, and they think the wedding should be today! What do you think?" Kim took Little Bird aside and said, "I know you aren't excited about this, but are you willing? If you're not, we'll stick with you."

She responded, "For the sake of my family, I'm willing."

Kim suggested a scroll painting of I Corinthians 13, the love chapter, as a gift. I presented it to the groom in front of everyone. An uncle read it out loud and translated it from Chinese to Nosu. I gave the young couple three minutes of marriage counseling and my blessing. An hour later they left on a 10-day trip to Sichuan province to complete the marriage ceremony at his parent's home.

We don't like arranged marriages. It makes the women seem like used cars (so, how many miles does she got on her?). But in a traditional culture where almost all marriages are arranged, the alternatives are also not attractive. It didn't take long after Little Bird's divorce before unsavory men were paying too much attention to her.

We don't like being forced to make decisions with inadequate information. I had spent more time on the internet researching granola recipes than I spent with the suitor.

A few months later, a pastor from our home church, Rick Lum, and his wife Tiz, came back to China to spend their sabbatical with us. Rick offered to do actual marriage counseling for the young couple and they accepted. He drew a triangle with their names and God's—one name at each of the three corners.

He explained that as they each move closer to God, they move closer to each other. They asked him to perform a Christian wedding ceremony.

They sent out invitations and about 200 people came. We had a team from Idaho helping with an English camp, and they learned a song in Nosu to perform at the wedding. Some of the guests who came in from the villages had never seen a foreigner before. When this group of 12 Americans, the women all wearing pleated Nosu skirts, came up front and sang in Nosu, the villagers' jaws dropped. Rick explained the gospel and its impact on marriages (through an interpreter). Little Bird and her husband said their vows. Music pumped and the celebration went on.

Little Bird's life and soul were in good hands.

With this ring...

25 RONTU

"Poignance is ten cents a ton. 'If we need poignance', I said, 'we'll kill the family dog.' I hate poignance." Patrick McManus, "The Deer on a Bicycle"

Rontu's self-esteem was off the charts. We had bought him out of a three-wheeled cart for a few dollars, and the kids lavished attention on him and took him everywhere.

He was a Lhasa terrier mix, about 12 pounds, short legs, big chest, teeth sticking out everywhere, bad eyes, perpetually dirty and bloody. He went through life like Russell Westbrook in an NBA playoff game, with an aggressive sneer and irrational self-confidence.

I saw him attack a Tibetan mastiff—literally 10 times his weight—for no reason, then look disgustedly at me for bailing him out so he wouldn't die in glory. He would sidle up to leggy female dogs, smile at their knees, and say, "I'm here now, babe, thanks for waiting." Our neighborhood was filled with ugly short-legged puppies that had his color pattern.

Rontu would come into restaurants with us and walk from table to table, not begging, just checking to see if someone would give him a rib. We took him on the city buses and he learned to ride them by himself. People would tell us, "We saw your dog over by the monastery yesterday, on the bus." He would go up and down the aisles in the supermarket, and we would pretend we didn't know him.

The day Rontu went missing I hated China. The night before had been Chinese New Year, and people set off a small war's worth of fireworks. Rontu disappeared and didn't come back. Our kids were little, loved their dog like any good kids anywhere, and wanted me to do something. I printed out "Lost Dog – Y50 Reward!" papers (in Chinese of course) and posted them all over town.

As I went through hanging the posters I hated the noise and the dirt. I hated the way people followed us around and paid attention to everything we did. I hated the stupid way people said "Halloo?!" to us and laughed, like they were the first person to ever think of saying that to a foreigner, instead of the 1.3 billionth person. I hated the way they laughed at my lost dog posters. I hated the fireworks and the superstition and having to use earplugs and MP3 players to sleep through the night. I hated that Anna and Niels were growing up not being able to go to church and be on the skit team, or be in kids' choir, or play Little League baseball, or learn to ski, or be normal. I hated that some people at home felt like I was begging for money to pay my salary. I hated arranged marriages and women being treated like commodities and smug 8th grade husbands. I hated that the people in charge, the Chinese, treated the minorities like simpletons—only good for singing and dancing and looking picturesque. I hated that Kim and I couldn't figure out how to do language study without arguing about it.

I didn't want Rontu to be gone because someone got drunk and felt like killing a dog, or because someone was driving like an idiot and ran over him, or because someone stole him because he belonged to the foreigners. I loved Rontu and his cockiness, maybe because he seemed like an American and I was homesick.

I never mentioned to Kim or the kids or our local friends or in our newsletters how much I hated living in China sometimes. It wasn't every day—only on bad days, which were pretty rare. But on the day Rontu was gone, if God would have given me the deal, "I'll blow up the other half of town, and you get your dog back," I would have taken the dog in a heartbeat.

The next afternoon Rontu kicked in the door, said "hi" to the kids, and went to sleep under the stove. The other side of town was unharmed. But we were in year six of a three-year plan, we wanted Anna and Niels to spend some of their high school years in the US, I had had a bellyful of living in China, and I was ready to go home.

Rontu dressed as Emperor Nero. It was his idea.

26 A COME TO JESUS MOMENT

Indeed Bilbo found that he had lost more than spoons – he had lost his reputation. J.R.R. Tolkien, The Hobbit

I loved the clean air and quiet nights in Idaho. I found a job with Walsh Engineering that was a perfect fit. Niels and Anna found new dogs, friends, and activities. Kim found that it was a relief to not study Chinese every day.

Church had always been a big part of my life, but now I went primarily to play ultimate Frisbee. I had been a leader, served on the elder board, and even preached occasionally. But after returning my reputation was reduced to The China Guy. Conversations in the hallway often started, "So, when do you head back to China?" I dreaded it. I still went every Sunday, with the same self-discipline that took me to my annual dental cleanings. But I came in five minutes late and shot out the back door after the closing prayer to play ultimate Frisbee with the teenagers to avoid the hallway conversations.

Instead of going to church with an attitude that was worshipful and teachable, I sat through it like Simon Cowell judging a talent competition, and commented later on the competencies of the song leaders and preachers. I was on my way to becoming a cynical bore.

A couple of people at church made the same joke, or perhaps it was an objective observation: "I wish you had stayed in China. Your newsletters were more interesting than you are in person."

We had been sent by our church to do our work in China, and they did a tremendous job in supporting us—sending teams, money, and encouragement. Why would returning be so hard?

• I had a sense I had failed to live up to the expectations of our church members. I suspected that in the disagreements about ministry methodology I had had with Kim, she had been right all along and I had let my stubbornness prevent me from doing my job well.

• Although our financial supporters were great and I loved them, and I agreed with the concept of financially supported ministry, I was weary of living off of others' donations. There was a wall in the back of our church with photos of the families that receive financial support, and it was a joy and a relief to me when our photo came down.

• Much like someone returning home after time in the military, I had invested years in developing knowledge and skills that were abruptly 100% irrelevant.

• My own spiritual disciplines, like Bible study and prayer, were erratic and dry. All I really wanted to do was work in my engineering job or in my garden, but not to let God work on me. It is hard to enjoy being at church when you are trying to keep the God you are worshipping at arm's length.

One Sunday a couple of years[32] after we returned, Kaiti shifted the microphone anxiously from hand to hand, as her father shuffled the sheet music at the piano. Now she is a polished performer, but when she was an 11-year-old in front of the church, Kaiti was nervous. She began,

Weak and wounded sinner
Lost and left to die
O, raise your head, for love is passing by
Come to Jesus
Come to Jesus
Come to Jesus and live!

Sitting in my normal seat at church, west side of the

---

[32] Two years is a wearisome long time to be a cynical bore. Sorry everyone!

auditorium, six rows from the front, I began to cry.

Now your burden's lifted
And carried far away
And precious blood has washed away the stain, so
Sing to Jesus
Sing to Jesus
Sing to Jesus and live!

A couple verses in, Kaiti was no longer nervous, and her childlike voice was sweet and powerful. Tears were dripping off of my nose.

And like a newborn baby
Don't be afraid to crawl
And remember when you walk
Sometimes we fall, so
Fall on Jesus
Fall on Jesus
Fall on Jesus and live!

I had fallen plenty. I had criticized heroic missionaries behind their backs, discouraged my wife, worn out my friends, stopped being grateful to my Savior.

Sometimes the way is lonely
And steep and filled with pain
So if your sky is dark and pours the rain, then
Cry to Jesus
Cry to Jesus
Cry to Jesus and live!

Tears weren't just falling from my eyes. Water, or maybe blood, was washing over my desiccated soul.

O, and when the love spills over
And music fills the night
And when you can't contain your joy inside, then
Dance for Jesus
Dance for Jesus
Dance for Jesus and live!
And with your final heartbeat
Kiss the world goodbye
Then go in peace, and laugh on Glory's side, and
Fly to Jesus

Fly to Jesus
Fly to Jesus and live!
Fly to Jesus
Fly to Jesus
Fly to Jesus and live!

I wasn't defined by successes or failures in China, or anywhere else. I was defined by being forgiven and free. I had come back to Jesus.

27 RE-ENGAGEMENT

"In history, the moments during which reason and reconciliation prevail are short and fleeting." Stefan Zweig

"Kim, I'm sorry I couldn't be the hero you wanted me to be in China." I didn't say it in a way that was a real apology. What I meant was that her expectations had been irrationally high, and, if we disagreed about it, it was her fault.

She knew exactly what I meant and she snapped back, "Don't use the 'H' word with me. I never wanted that; I just wanted you to actually listen to me when I had something to say."

We had been back in Idaho for five years. Our relationships with our kids, our families, our church, our co-workers, our friends, and even our new dogs were near perfect. But we still couldn't talk about China. We were on mile one of a 10 mile hike near the Tetons. At mile five we were yelling at each other[33]. At mile nine we were walking 50 feet apart, not talking. Most of the time the rift that had opened 10 years before was closed on the surface, but, like an infected sliver, every now and then some pus would squeeze out. We could go back to our happy American lives and kind of pretend China never happened. But the infection was still there under the surface.

---

[33] Silver lining: from my research, no one has ever surprised a grizzly while they were in a high volume marital argument.

Finally I asked for two months off of work. Kim and I arranged to stay at a cabin in northern Idaho, without a TV or internet connection, and try to extract that infected sliver. We decided we would put no limits on the time we would spend talking, or the relational pain we were willing to endure.

We walked about 40 miles a week on the trails around Lake Coeur d' Alene and talked. We drank box wine in the evening and talked. We drove to see our kids at the University of Idaho and talked in the car. We had arguments that resulted in us walking 50 feet apart. We held hands on the couch and prayed together almost every evening. I literally prayed that if we had brought a demon back with us in our baggage that was preventing us from being reconciled, that it would be exorcised. We went to bed, got up, ate more oatmeal, and went walking and talking again.

I realized I made decisions quickly and firmly, and Kim needed to talk them out. When we had discussed entering language school, or enrolling Anna and Niels in Chinese public school, I had made a "no" decision in about 10 minutes. I thought Kim was nagging by continuing to bring something up that "we" had already decided on. She thought I didn't listen to her and was peremptory and impatient. There wasn't a singular conversation of resolution, but after many miles and hours and tears, we realized that the sliver had popped out. We could see from each other's perspective and forgive[34].

We decided to re-engage with our friends in China, not so much for their benefit as for our own. I asked for more time off and we bought tickets.

Just like it had almost 25 years ago, China smelled like charcoal smoke, diesel exhaust, burnt red peppers, and old urine. When I got off the plane, a flood of memories returned, most of them good.

On the first night we arrived at our old home, about 20 of our Nosu friends threw a party for us. There was a gratifying amount of tears and laughter. They killed a pig for us. Normally we only rated a chicken, but we hadn't been there for five years.

---

[34] Describing it, all this seems absurdly simple, like it should have taken 10 minutes to figure out, not 10 years. (Whoops, there I go again.)

For two weeks we ate and laughed and played with the kids. A seven-year-old asked, "Uncle, what is the happiest thing in your life?"

"I suppose having a nice meal with family and friends. What is the happiest thing in your life?"

"When you and Auntie Kim are here."

Kim and I went for walks every day. We weren't walking 50 feet apart; we were holding hands. The sliver was gone and the wound was healed. Our metaphorical and possibly real demons were gone.

As we walked we reflected on the changes we had seen in China since our first trip there. The sustained economic change had been unlike anything in history[35]. Numerically, the annual per capita GDP had gone from $500 to over $8,000. Personally, when Little Bird was a pre-school kid in the mountains, she was often hungry, hoping someone in the clan would put an arrow in a monkey so they could eat something besides aging potatoes that night. Twenty-five years later, she was using her phone to order new shoes from TaoBao.com, while driving her minivan, while putting on Clinique dark spot corrector makeup with her free hand.

The worldview changes have been as dramatic as the economic. Ideological communism is a relic, like a rusting statue of Chairman Mao. Traditionally insular cultures like the Nosu are swimming in a tidal wave of new ideas. There is significant risk and opportunity.

As Christians, Kim and I hoped that the Nosu, and groups like them worldwide, would consider following Jesus. If Christianity is true, it is the only option that will complete the culture and let it function in its full unique beauty. If you think cultures always change that way when they become Christian, perfectly and beautifully, you are not good at history. But if you think Christianity only disdains and damages traditional cultures, you are even worse.

We had time for these profound conversations, as we didn't

---

[35] By comparison, if you go to Plummer, Idaho, my hometown, it looks almost the same as it did in 1993. The houses are the same, and the same Buicks are up on the same cinderblocks.

have phones or an internet connection where we stayed. One day, feeling responsible to check in with my long-suffering employer, who had given me another two-month leave, we hiked three miles to town to check our email in a coffee shop.

The email conversation, paraphrased:

Kim's mother, Emily: There is an emergency, please call me.

Kim: Sorry, I can't call you, please email me.

Emily: Sorry to tell you this by email, but your dad died this morning.

Gary was 73, in excellent health, and his death came as a complete surprise. Kim took 30 minutes to compose herself, then, while I made emergency travel arrangements, she used his death as an opportunity to gather our Nosu friends and speak about ultimate issues. Nothing she could have done would have made Gary more proud.

After a five-hour ride in a tiny Chinese minivan, three hastily arranged flights, and a 10-hour drive in a rental car, we arrived in Idaho.

It had been almost 25 years since our first trip to China. We left like we were fleeing from a crime, or hurrying to a funeral. We have no plans to return.

This past summer, on the 24th day of the 6th lunar month, on the date of the torch festival, 100 of us built a spectacular bonfire in our church's parking lot in Idaho Falls. We thanked God for his kindness to us and to the Nosu, and for our friendships. And the mountains echoed with our celebration.

EPILOGUE

Ahma still sells merchandise in the town square and laughs with her head thrown back.

Diji will graduate from college next year and is engaged. Anna plans to attend her wedding.

Zeyi is a 20-year-old college student, intelligent and poised. When he saw me last year he gave me a big hug and said, "Thank you for what you did for me when I was little."

Teacher Lu, the Nosu Renaissance Man, has retired and lives in the same mountainous village where I met him.

Rontu, after a long and legendary career as a lover and a fighter, died of old age.

Kim taught ESL in Idaho Falls for several years and hosted some amazing Latino potluck dinners. She has retired from teaching and is currently writing a book, which will be much longer and better than this one.

Little Bird has two more beautiful daughters. The youngest is on the cover of this book. After a six-year silence, she was allowed to see Hope and Lydia. They didn't recognize her. The girls live with their father's family and attend one of the village boarding schools.

The church in China has continued to grow, including among the Nosu people.

Anna is 22 now, with a college degree, a husband, and many Chinese friends. She is still mildly annoyed about her stuffed animals being stolen.

Niels is a 20-year-old pre-med student. He would still rather go fishing than play computer games.

I have come to peace about being The China Guy. I even wrote a book about it.

I asked Niels and Anna for a short description of what they remember about growing up in China.

Niels: I was six years old when we moved to China. Young people are malleable, so I adapted quickly. I did not find it odd or upsetting that we took dump showers, or that we had no refrigerator, or that we bought a year's supply of cocoa powder and cinnamon each time we returned to Idaho Falls. "This is just what we do," I thought. "This is my life."

Every evening we heated water in a giant copper teapot on our iron woodstove. We would pour the boiling water into four battered Nalgene bottles, and each take one to bed with us to heat our frigid sleeping bags.

I remember playing sports constantly. To be fair, I still do this. But the combination of my elementary school exuberance and a bunch of eager Chinese and Tibetan neighbor kids made a perfect scene for pick-up basketball, soccer, and bike races.

We ate out often. The grimy hole-in-the-wall restaurants in our town served food that was far cheaper than any fast food and much tastier than any sit-down place you could find in the States. The greasy hash brown style potatoes, the spicy breaded pork ribs, or the cold cucumbers with soy sauce and cayenne—I loved them all.

I always felt safe with the people in China. Anna and I often rode the public bus across town, and I explored the alleyways of the traditional old town with my friends. People were friendly and open and kind, and I trusted them. The only time I ever got lost, an elderly farmer led me back across the barley fields to the friend's house we were staying in.

I remember spending time with Zeyi. He was the best friend I ever had, and he came when I needed him most. We didn't share the same first language, culture, or skin color, but what we did share was more significant than what we didn't. We shot baskets for hours on end, shared meals—sometimes at his house and sometimes at ours—and pretended to do homework together when his grandmother was paying attention. Sometimes Ahma would introduce us as brothers, and we liked it best that way.

Anna: I remember food, friendship, and fear. In case you're wondering, I didn't sit and arrange my thoughts to fit the alliteration. Those words are what came to mind first so I kept them.

I couldn't even handle black pepper on my scrambled eggs before I lived in China. Because of dishes like *gongbaojiding*, *ganbanyanyusi*, *mapodofu*, and several unidentifiable vacuum-sealed snacks, I learned that pain can be well worth the flavor of the food it's in. Now I can take my spice *almost* as well as Diji can. When I miss China the most, food is often a substantial part of that longing. And I marvel that God decided to make food interact with our taste buds in a way that brings us delight.

To this day I have a disproportionate appreciation of peanut butter and Vanilla Coke. We couldn't buy them from anywhere closer than nine hours away, so we hoarded and savored them. That first scoop into the smooth top of a new jar of peanut butter is still magical.

I spent a lot of my time lonely. I prayed for an English-speaking girl my age to live in our town so I could have a best friend there, and God answered in unexpected ways. He gave me Diji. He brought my Idaho Falls friends even closer to me through emails and Yahoo chat on Saturday mornings. I'm not sure if He meant for me to become such close friends with a cat, but Lymrik arrived at our home at two weeks old and I took his companionship and ran with it. Also, Mom told me, "You and Niels can be best friends or enemies, and you decide that now," and I slowly but intentionally started seeing Niels as a friend. Now I treasure our relationship highly. In hindsight, I've learned that I should have held God as my closest friend. He would have filled the hole in my heart to overflowing.

There were a couple kinds of fear. Neither were of physical harm; I felt safer in our little town than I have anywhere else in the world. The first was of people. With my fair skin, blond hair and blue eyes, and tall nose, I looked so different from the locals that most people couldn't help but stare. I took it personally and developed a fear of people noticing me in any context. I still sometimes blush when someone chooses to talk to me, because they *see me*.

The other fear I remember was not like most American childhood fears: of social situations, new experiences, or scary animals like sharks and spiders. Where we lived, kids were afraid of ghosts and demons. Adults were too. There, spiritual beings were as real (or more) than what we could see with our eyes. I spent a lot of time whispering to beings in the darkness that Jesus is my Lord, He is more powerful than them, and they can do nothing to harm me. I am still completely sure that there are beings bent on human destruction, but my fear has decreased as I've learned the overwhelming power of the God who created us and *sees us* and is working everything so that He will win, we will live forever in His love, and all of it will shout His glory.

Niels and Anna in 2017.

LESSONS LEARNED

"In the case of significant conditions adverse to quality, the cause of the condition shall be determined and corrective action taken to prevent recurrence."

NQA-1, Basic Requirement 16

One of our extended family members who has gone through rehab therapy likes to say, "The important thing is that you have learned from your experiences." So here is a summary of what I have learned from our experience going, living, and coming back from China.

1. In Chinese, if you don't know the tone, you don't know the word.

2. You probably won't do dramatically different things overseas than you have done at home. If you have never planted a church or an organic garden plot at home, don't expect that a plane trip will enable you to plant one in a different country.

3. Pray for your kids.

4. If you have an on-going issue in your marriage, it probably won't be resolved without some pain. Resolving it will be worth the cost.

5. You'll probably never live overseas unless you get out of debt first. I have described the financial aspect of going overseas in some detail not because it is the most important consideration, but because it is a limiting factor for many young families. If you have no way to get out of debt you are obligated to keep working to pay the debts. The borrower is slave to the lender.

The most common ways I have seen for people to

voluntarily[36] get in over their head financially are:

- getting a low value college degree financed primarily by student loans (think Irish Studies from Strayer University at $31,000 per year)
- spending too much on a car
- spending too much on a house (I know, you are a Christian, and you *need* 4000 sq. ft. for hosting a Bible study once a month, so I'll get off your case.)
- going nuts on a hobby (men only).

If you can avoid these four mistakes, you can buy the good ketchup every time you grocery shop, be generous when opportunities arise, and still be out of debt when you feel led to move overseas.

6. Re-entry after spending years overseas is complex and difficult. If you are good friends with someone who has returned, please be patient with them.

---

[36] I'm not referring to someone who has involuntary expenses, like taking care of a parent or special needs child. If that is your situation, you are a better person than me, and I'm not giving you advice.

NOTES ON SOURCES

Nosu:
A Journey through South-West Sechuen, by Edward Amundsen, *The Geographical Journal*, Vol. 16, No. 5. (Nov., 1900), pp. 531-537

"The Lolos and Other Tribes of Western China," by A. Henry, *The Journal of the Anthropological Institute of Great Britain and Ireland*, Vol. 33. (Jan. - Jun., 1903), pp. 96-107

"The Lolo of Szechuan Province, China," by D. C. Graham, *American Anthropologist*, New Series, Vol. 32, No. 4. (Oct. - Dec., 1930), pp. 703-705

The Historical Origins of The Lolo, by Feng Han-Yi; J. K. Shryock, *Harvard Journal of Asiatic Studies*, Vol. 3, No. 2. (Jul., 1938), pp. 103-127.

"Frontier Tribes of Southwest China," by Hsien-Chin Hu, *Far Eastern Survey*, Vol. 11, No. 10. (May 18, 1942), pp. 116-120.

"Kinship System of The Lolo," by Lin Yueh-hwa, *Harvard Journal of Asiatic Studies*, Vol. 9, No. 2. (Jun., 1946), pp. 81-100

"Marriage Among the Independent Lolos of Western China," by Siang-Feng Ko, *The American Journal of Sociology*, Vol. 54, No. 6. (May, 1949), pp. 487-496

"Captives, Kin, and Slaves in Xiao Liangshan," by Ann Maxwell Hill, *The Journal of Asian Studies*, Vol. 60, No. 4. (Nov., 2001), pp. 1033-1049.

Traditional Nuosu Origin Narratives: A Case Study of Ritualized Epos in Bimo Incantation Scriptures, by Bamo Qubumo

"Ethnicity, Local Interests, and the State: Yi Communities in Southwest China," by Stevan Harrell, *Comparative Studies in Society and History*, Vol. 32, No. 3. (Jul., 1990), pp. 515-548.

"Sino-Tibetan Linguistics: Present State and Future Prospects," by James A. Matisoff, *Annual Review of Anthropology*, Vol. 20. (1991), pp. 469-504

"The History of the History of the Yi, Part II," by Stevan Harrell and Li Yongxiang, *Modern China*, Vol. 29, No. 3. (Jul.,

2003), pp. 362-396

"Ethnic Entrepreneurship and Ethnic Identity: A Case Study among the Liangshan Yi (Nuosu) in China," by Thomas Heberer, *The China Quarterly*, 2005

"Tribes of Snow: Animals and Plants in the Nuosu Book of Origins," by Mark Bender, *Asian Ethnology*, Spring 2008

Strong Man's Prey, by Dr. James Broomhall, China Inland Mission, 1953

Mission Impossible, by Ralph Covell Hope, 1990

Liberating Gospel in China, by Ralph Covell, Baker, 1995

Mountain Patterns: The Survival of Nuosu Culture, by Stevan Harrel, Bamo Ayi, Ma Lunzy, University of Washington Press, 2000

Perspectives on the Yi of Southwest China, by Stevan Harrel, University of California Press, 2001

Ways of Being Ethnic in SW China, by Stevan Harrel, University of Washington Press, 2002

Nuosu Yi Chinese English Glossary, by Walters, Walters, and Ma, Minzu Chubanshe Nationalities Publishing House, 2008

Tibetans:
Discussion of CIA training of Tibetans from *Buddha's Warriors* - The Story of the CIA-Backed Tibetan Freedom Fighters, the Chinese Invasion, and the Ultimate Fall of Tibet, by Mikel Dunham, Penguin, 2004

Christianity in China:
Eternity in Their Hearts, by Don Richardson, Regal Books, 1981

Discussion of Chinese Christians influence on China's economic surge from *Jesus in Beijing*, by David Aikman, Regnery Publishing, 2003.

Operation World, Patrick Johnstone, OM Publishing, 2000

Music:
Lyrics to "Come to Jesus," Chris Rice, Warner/Chappell Music.

ABOUT THE COVER AND THE AUTHOR

The cover: On our last visit, Little Bird's youngest daughter was at the cutest age of little-girl bossiness. "Uncle, you stand here! Don't move! Shut your eyes!" And so on. But one day she had a request instead of command. "Uncle, will you get your biggest camera and take pictures of *me*?" I only took a few, but the one on the cover represents to me the exuberant hope the Nosu people have for their future.

Nosu art typically uses red, black, and yellow, so I used it for the cover text and back cover border. The Chinese 山友 is a loose translation of the book's title. The photo of me on the back cover is with five cousins who have just worked me over in some high-altitude basketball.

The author: I[37] grew up a long ways from the nearest neighbor, in the north Idaho woods, on the Coeur d' Alene Indian reservation, prior to graduating from the University of Idaho. I've made at least a few hundred dollars by logging, tying trout flies, splitting cedar fence rails, driving a forklift, doing standup comedy while juggling, tutoring physics, teaching ESL, and electrical engineering. I hope to add writing a short book in only seven years to that list.

You can reach me by emailing labtoes@yahoo.com.

---

[37] It was tempting to write the "About the Author" section in the third person, to create the illusion that I have a publicist.

CPSIA information can be obtained
at www.ICGtesting.com
Printed in the USA
LVHW080127210622
721738LV00027B/893